North American
INDIAN POINTS

Identification & Value Guide

ISBN 0-89689-044-9

Copyright © 1984 Books Americana Inc., Florence, Alabama 35630. All rights reserved. No part of the book may be used or reproduced in any manner whatsoever without permission, except in the case of brief quotations embodied in critical articles or reviews.

INTRODUCTION

Fascination with things American Indian is deeply ingrained in our culture. It began with childhood games, Cowboys and Indians. It is continually reinforced by advertising symbols, company names, movies, television, everyday conversation.

No American needs to ask the meaning of these phrases: "Burying the hatchet"; "Smoke the peacepipe"; "Indian Summer". And how many low-ranking military personnel have complained about "Too many chiefs, not enough Indians"? The American Indian or Amerind presence is everywhere, and a healthy part of our national existence.

This partly explains the present fascination with objects made by Indians. There are today probably well over one million persons who collect Indian goods or are in other ways involved in this vast area.

There are certain characteristics of Amerind collectibles. One is that they are almost always made from natural materials and substances, whether plant, animal or mineral. Another is that all, or almost all, of the work required to complete the object is done by hand, slowly and carefully.

Yet another characteristic is workstyle, with the object being shaped into a form familiar to the Amerind lifeways. It is decorated, if at all, with designs that have their origin in the timeless North American past.

The essence of the Amerind art form — be it utensil, tool, weapon, ornament, whatever — is uniqueness. For all authentic pieces there was, and is, no such "improvement" as assembly-line mass production. And no two objects are ever totally alike, no matter how much they may resemble one another. The pieces are as varied as the individuals that made them; each is a sole creation.

Perhaps still another hallmark of Amerind works, and one that appeals highly to collectors, is the "utility-plus" factor. A great percentage of Amerind objects were made far better than necessary to merely complete a task. Much loving skill and attention to detail were added.

Amerind art and artifacts have long been admired and collected in European countries and elsewhere. Americans, pioneer and recent, have largely failed to understand or appreciate the field. Only within the last few years has there been a broad groundswell of interest and attention, but Americans have now begun to accept good Amerind material as good art.

Native American art, sometimes primitive, sometimes amazingly sophisticated, has gone (in regard to marketability) far beyond the flash and fad stages. It has become a major field to be in, a heritage to be knowledgeable about, **the** collectibles to have.

Some preliminary explanations and comments are in order. There are terms used throughout this Guide that are important. "Prehistoric" means before-writing, or the arrival of Europeans to record events. Prehistoric also means cultural items designed by Amerinds alone, without ideological contamination from European sources and generally this means all human-occupied North American time **before** about AD 1500.

"Historic", as used here, means heavy cultural contact with Europeans and Russians, in a time zone broadly ranging from AD 1500 to AD 1900. "Recent", is here considered to be from 1900 to 1970. "Contemporary" indicates year from 1970 to the present. These time-zones are open to debate, but if the meaning is clear they remain sufficient and descriptive.

This book is a **Guide** to American Indian Points and their values. It identifies and describes major collecting areas available today. Representative prices, or close price ranges, are accurately given.

It should be noted that the listed value — whether for item description or photograph — is not an ultimate valuation. It does not usually constitute an offer to sell. It does not represent an appraisal. Instead, it is judged by the possessor to be a fair market value.

While the Guide should be a general help in acquiring good pieces at reasonable prices, there is yet no substitute for personal knowledge and experience. The more you know about what you decide to collect, the better will be your point collection.

WEST OF MISSISSIPPI

ABASOLO: 5000 to 3000 B.C.

Description: This is a leaf-shaped point having straight to slightly convex side edges and a rounded basal edge. Some points are beveled on the side edges indicating they were sometimes used as knives as well as dart points. This point is closely related to Tortugas points which have straight basal edges and are also beveled.

Distribution: It is commonly found in the lower Rio Grande Valley, southern Texas, and northeastern Mexico.

.75-1.00

WEST OF MISSISSIPPI

ABILENE: 5000 to 3000 B.C.

Description: This is a medium sized dart point with convex edges. The blade is narrow, thick, and leaf-shaped. Stem edges are usually beveled to the right. Basal edge may be concave, straight or convex. Flaking is crude.

Distribution: Central Texas and surrounding areas.

1.00-2.00

WEST OF MISSISSIPPI

AFTON: 3500 to 500 B.C.

Description: This is a large, corner-notched point having an angular blade outline, square to pointed barbs, and a short, expanded stem. They are usually thin and well made. It is thought to belong to the Late Archaic period in Oklahoma. The Jacks Reef point in Ohio and farther east is similar in form but smaller and later in time.

Distribution: Afton points are found in eastern Oklahoma and in the nearby states of Kansas and Missouri.

2.50-3.00

WEST OF MISSISSIPPI

AGATE BASIN: 7500 to 7000 B.C.

Description: These are long, slender, lanceolate points being widest in the upper one-third to one-half of the points. Chipping technique may be random, or they may have parallel flaking. Most have straight to slightly concave basal edges, rarely a convex basal edge. Edges of the stems are ground from one-fourth to nearly one-third their length. They are considered Early Archaic points in some areas, Late Paleo points in other areas.

Distribution: They are found in the Midwest, in Arkansas and Oklahoma, and in the Plains from Texas to Canada.

20.00-30.00

WEST OF MISSISSIPPI

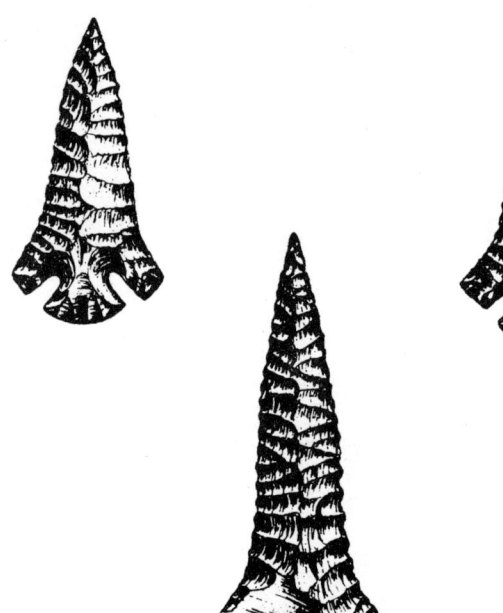

AGEE: A.D. 700 to 1000

Description: These are corner-notched arrow points having recurved blades and fan-shaped stems. Notches are U-shaped to V-shaped, barbs are squared to pointed. Flaking consists of carefully controlled pressure flaking over the entire point. Later Caddoan arrow points of the Hayes, Alba and Catahoula types may be descendants of the Agee points.

Distribution: These points are found on Coles Creek and related Late Woodland sites in southwestern Arkansas, southeastern Oklahoma, and northeastern Texas.

2.00-2.50

WEST OF MISSISSIPPI

ALBA: A.D. 900 to 1300

Description: These arrow points have triangular to recurved blades and parallel-sided to bulbous or fan-shaped stems. Barbs are usually sharp. Some points may be finely serrated or have needle-like tips. These points seem to be a direct descendant of the Agee points in the area.

Distribution: The points were made by Caddoan Indians located in eastern Oklahoma, western Arkansas, northeastern Louisiana, and northeastern Texas.

1.50-2.00

WEST OF MISSISSIPPI

ALBERTA: 7000 to 5000 B.C.

Description: This is a medium to large dart point with sides that are slightly convex and parallel. The blade is rounded and leaf-shaped with a blunted tip. The base is wide and rectangular with a concave base. The point is rare.

Distribution: West of the Mississippi River.

20.00-25.00

WEST OF MISSISSIPPI

ALLEN: 6000 to 4000 B.C.

Description: This is a medium size dart or spear point having concave edges that tend to be parallel toward the base. The blade is thin & lanceolate shaped. The base is concave and the base corners are rounded. The chipping is of the parallel oblique type. This point is scarce.

Distribution: It is found in Wyoming mostly.

7.50-10.00

WEST OF MISSISSIPPI

AVONLEA: A.D. 200 to 600

Description: This is a triangular arrow point having convex sides and low, shallow side-notches. The basal edge is concave and rarely straight. Grinding has been noted on the basal edge of some points. It is one of the earliest arrow points known in North America and is presumed to have been made by Athabascan peoples migrating southward into the United States.

Distribution: It is found on the northern plains in the Dakotas, Montana, and the Canadian provinces of Alberta, Saskatchewan, and Manitoba.

1.00-1.50

WEST OF MISSISSIPPI

BASSETT: A.D. 1300 to 1600

Description: This is a triangular arrow point having two basal notches that form a short pointed stem in the center of the base. Some points are serrated and may have needle-like tips. These Late Caddoan points are found in numbers along the Red River between Texarkana and Shreveport.

Distribution: It is found in northwestern Louisiana, southwestern Arkansas, northeastern Texas, and southeastern Oklahoma, and was made by Caddoan Indians of the Fulton Aspect.

1.00-1.50

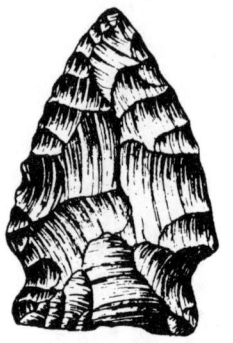

BESANT: A.D. 100 to 500

Description: This is a small, convex-sided dart point having wide, shallow side-notches, and a straight to slightly convex basal edge. While the point is a side-notched type, the base is generally narrower than the shoulders which are angular. Besant points are a product of Middle Woodland peoples.

Distribution: These points are found primarily in Canada in the provinces of Saskatchewan and Alberta, but also occur in the northern United States in Montana and the Dakotas.

.50-.75

WEST OF MISSISSIPPI

BLANCO: 30,000 B.C.

Description: This is a small, pointed oval shaped blade. It could possibly be one of the earliest points and because of this will show intense weathering. It is crudely chipped and shows no retouching. These points are rare.

Distribution: They are found in South America, Mexico, New Mexico, and Texas.

20.00-30.00

WEST OF MISSISSIPPI

BONHAM: A.C. 700 to 1200

Description: This is a small arrow point having a narrow, rectangular stem. Sides may be concave, convex, or recurved. Stem ends may be squared or rounded. Barbs are short and pointed. The Alba point has a similar form but wider stem.

Distribution: The type is found in north-central and northeastern Texas, southern Oklahoma, and southwestern Arkansas. It was made by Caddoan peoples. A similar point was made earlier by Late Woodland peoples.

1.00-1.50

WEST OF MISSISSIPPI

BRECKENRIDGE: 7500 to 7000 B.C.

Description: This is a medium to large-size point having broad, shallow side-notches and an expanded base. The basal edge is concave. Most points have become beveled when sharpened. Some points have beveled notches. This is one of the many forms of Dalton points known to exist and probably served as a knife.

Distribution: They are found in the Ozark mountain area of Missouri and in the Ouachita Mountain areas of Arkansas and Oklahoma, and were made by Early Archaic peoples.

8.00-9.00

WEST OF MISSISSIPPI

BULVERDE: 3000 B.C. to A.D. 500

Description: This is a medium to large dart point having straight to convex sides, a rectangular stem and barbed shoulders. The basal edge is straight. It has a random flaking pattern with wide, flat flakes having been removed overall. The Bulverde point is similar to the Little River point found in southeastern Oklahoma and southwestern Arkansas.

Distribution: It is primarily found in central Texas. Similar points are found in eastern Oklahoma and western Arkansas, but their affiliation, if any, has not been established.

1.00-1.50

WEST OF MISSISSIPPI

CACHE RIVER: 7500 to 7000 B.C.

Description: This is a small to medium-size dart point. It is lanceolate in form, thin, and has narrow side-notches and a straight to concave basal edge. Some basal edges are lightly ground. Notches are narrow and some expand internally. Similar points of equal age are found in states north and east of northeastern Arkansas.

Distribution: Their major provenience is in the western lowlands of northeastern Arkansas. They occur in smaller numbers in southern and southwestern Arkansas, and in southeastern Oklahoma.

2.00-2.50

WEST OF MISSISSIPPI

CALF CREEK: 4000 to 3000 B.C.

Description: This is a broad, medium-size point having convex sides when new, and basal notches. The notches are narrow and often deep. Stems are parallel to slightly expanding. Some stem edges are lightly ground. Serrations occur on blade edges of some point. Most specimens are discards having been resharpened often thus losing some, or all, of the barbs. They evidently served as knives.

Distribution: They are found in southern Missouri, Arkansas, eastern Oklahoma, and northeastern Texas.

10.00-11.00

WEST OF MISSISSIPPI

CARROLLTON: 2000 to 1000 B.C.

Description: A small to medium dart point having straight to slightly convex edges and a triangular blade. The stem is ⅓ to ½ of the length of the point with prominent shoulders. It has irregular and crude workmanship.

Distribution: The Carrollton point is found mostly in Texas.

1.00-3.00

WEST OF MISSISSIPPI

CASTROVILLE: 3000 to 500 B.C.

Description: This is a medium to large, triangular point having medium-deep basal notches. The edges of the blade are straight, the basal edge is slightly convex. Notches enter on the curved basal edge to form an expanded stem. Barbs are often squared, rarely pointed. It is similar to the Williams point but is broader and was made on a preform having a convex basal edge.

Distribution: This point is found primarily in a wide area of central Texas oriented more north and south than east and west from the center of distribution. Points closely resembling them are found in Oklahoma.

2.00-2.50

WEST OF MISSISSIPPI

DALTON: 7500 to 6000 B.C.

Description: This is a small to medium-size point having recurved sides and concave, recurved basal edge. It is often serrated and beveled when resharpened. Basal edges are ground. Basal thinning is noted on most specimens. There are at least ten varieties of the Dalton point, some of which have been named such as the Breckenridge point.

Distribution: Dalton points are found in most states east of the Rockies. They are found in considerable numbers in northeastern and southwestern Arkansas.

7.00-9.50

DARL: 0 to A.D. 1000

Description: This is small, narrow dart point having convex sides, weak shoulders, and straight to expanded stems with straight to concave basal edges. Some points have beveled blade edges, some also have beveled stem edges. They are a product of Late Archaic peoples of the Edwards Plateau Aspect.

Distribution: They are found primarily in central and north-central Texas ranging northward into the adjoining portion of Oklahoma.

1.00-1.50

WEST OF MISSISSIPPI

DESMUKE: 4000 to 3000 B.C.

Description: This is a small to medium sized dart point having edges that are straight to convex. The point is thick and crudely made. The basal end of the stem is usually pointed. Sometimes the blade is beveled on one or both faces.

Distribution: Wide area of Central and Eastern United States.

.50-1.50

WEST OF MISSISSIPPI

DICKSON: 500 B.C. to A.D. 350

Description: This is a medium to large-size point having convex or recurved edges on the blade, angular shoulders and a contracting truncated stem. They are thin and well made. The flaking pattern is random, flake scars are broad and shallow. Some points in northwestern Arkansas and northeastern Oklahoma presently classified as Langtry points are Dickson points.

Distribution: They are found associated with Early and Middle Woodland sites in Ohio, Indiana, Illinois, Missouri, Iowa, Wisconsin, Michigan, northwestern Arkansas, northeastern Oklahoma, and southeastern Kansas.

3.00-3.50

WEST OF MISSISSIPPI

DUNCAN: 2500 to 850 B.C.

Description: This is a small, narrow dart point having convex sides and a straight to slightly expanding or contracting stem bifurcated on the basal edge. Shoulders are weak. Stem edges are usually ground. Duncan points are temporally related to Hanna and McKean points.

Distribution: They are found in Canada in the Provinces of Alberta and Saskatchewan, in Montana, the Dakotas, Wyoming, and Colorado. Similar points are found in Kansas and eastern Oklahoma.

3.50-4.00

WEST OF MISSISSIPPI

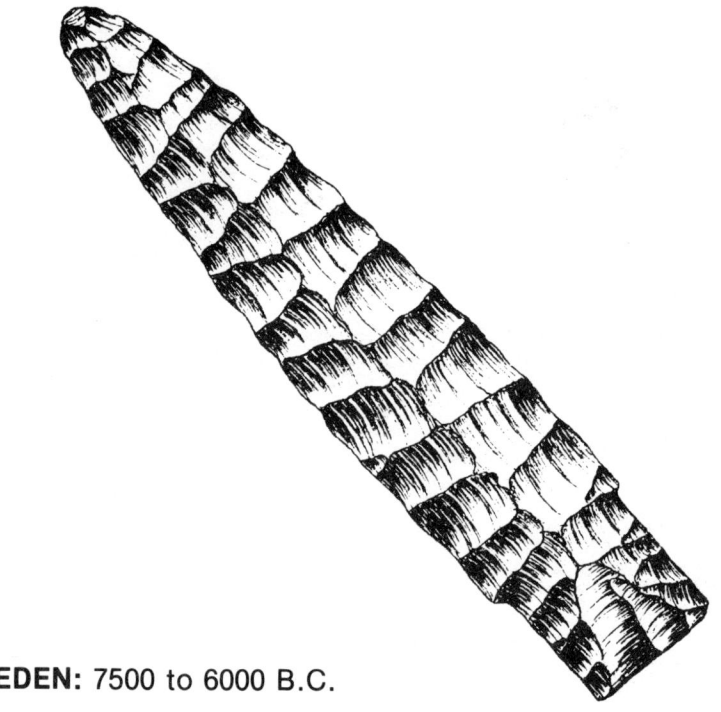

EDEN: 7500 to 6000 B.C.

Description: This is a long, narrow dart point having nearly parallel sides and a rectangular stem. Shoulders are weak to absent. Basal edges are usually straight, stem edges are smoothed by grinding. Flaking may be random or carefully spaced collaterally. Cross-sections may range from lenticular to diamond-shaped. The Eden point is sometimes found associated with Scottsbluff points in Nebraska, but not in the four corners area of Arkansas, Oklahoma, Texas, and Louisiana.

Distribution: They are found in the Plains area from southern Canada to Texas, and from the Rockies to eastern Oklahoma and Kansas. They are a product of Early Archaic Peoples.

20.00-22.00

WEST OF MISSISSIPPI

EDGEWOOD: 500 B.C. to A.D. 500

Description: This is a small dart point having an expanded stem and short barbs. Blade edges may be straight to convex; the basal edge is concave. The Ellis point is a variation having a straight basal edge.

Distribution: They are found primarily in southwestern Arkansas, southeastern Oklahoma, and in north-central and northeastern Texas.

1.00-1.50

WEST OF MISSISSIPPI

EDWARDS: A.D. 600 to 900

Description: This is an arrow point having prominent barbs on the shoulders and on the basal corners. Blade edges may be straight to convex. Notches are deep and narrow extending diagonally inward from the corners. The basal edge is V-shaped to concave. The earliest arrow points were usually smaller copies of preceding or contemporary dart points - in this case the Fairland point.

Distribution: They are found in the Edwards Plateau area of central Texas and were made by peoples corresponding, in time, to Late Woodland elsewhere. They are found associated with Fairland points.

2.00-2.50

WEST OF MISSISSIPPI

ELAM: 500 B.C. to 500 A.D.

Description: This is a small dart point having straight to convex edges. The blade is short and triangular with weak shoulders to almost absent and a rectangular stem. The basal edge is straight to slightly convex. The flaking is random with little or no retouching.

Distribution: Found mostly in the Central Texas area.

1.00-3.00

ENSOR: 1000 B.C. to A.D. 500

Description: This is a small to medium-size dart point having straight to convex sides and a short, expanding stem. The basal edge of the stem is straight, rarely concave or convex. Diagonal notches enter above the corners creating a wide stem and short barbs. This point may be a variant of, or related to, the Marcos points found in the same areas.

Distribution: It is found primarily in central Texas, but has been reported in sparse numbers in southern Oklahoma. It is found on Late Archaic and Woodland sites.

1.00-1.50

WEST OF MISSISSIPPI

ETLEY: 2000 to 500 B.C.

Description: This is a large spear point having a long blade and a short, rectangular or slightly expanding stem. The blade is recurved, concave from shoulder to ½ the length to point then parallel until about ¾ of the length and then concave to the tip. The basal edge is straight or slightly convex. The barbs point diagonally downward and away from the stem. This point is rare.

Distribution: The Etley point is found in Missouri, Illinois and the surrounding areas.

20.00-30.00

WEST OF MISSISSIPPI

EVANS: 800 to 600 B.C.

Description: This is a dart point having straight to convex sides and a square to expanded stem. Shoulders are lightly barbed. The basal edge may be straight or convex. A distinctive feature is a notch located one on each side of the blade a short distance above the shoulders. The point is expected to be a type in the Late Archaic-Early Woodland period.

Distribution: Evans points are found in northern Louisiana, southern Arkansas, and northeastern Texas.

5.00-5.50

WEST OF MISSISSIPPI

FOLSOM: 8000 B.C.

Description: This is a small to medium-size, lanceolate, fluted dart point. Its characteristics consist of wide, flat flutes often extending from the base to near the tips on both faces, a concave basal edge that may still retain evidence of the striking platform, and sharp barbed basal corners. Side edges may be straight to convex; basal edges are ground smooth. This is considered one of the latest of the fluted points.

Distribution: These points are found primarily on the Plains from Texas into Canada. In recent years small numbers have been found in west-central Illinois and in southern Wisconsin.

60.00-70.00

WEST OF MISSISSIPPI

FRESNO: A.D. 1400 to 1750

Description: This is a thin, slender, triangular arrow point having straight to slightly convex sides and a straight to slightly concave basal edge. Both faces are finely flaked and noticeable basal thinning occurs on some specimens. They differ from most Mississippian period points in that they are thinner and generally have sharper basal corners.

Distribution: The Fresno point is found in southern Arkansas, northern Louisiana, northeastern Texas, southeastern Kansas, and eastern Oklahoma, and was made by the Caddo and related groups.

.50-.75

WEST OF MISSISSIPPI

FRILEY: 1000 to 1500 A.D.

Description: This small bird point has a small, triangular blade with spurred shoulders projecting toward the tip. The stem and base are straight with the base maybe slightly convex or concave.

Distribution: This point is found in northwest Louisiana and surrounding areas.

2.00-5.00

WEST OF MISSISSIPPI

FRIO: 1000 B.C. to A.D. 500

Description: This is a medium-size dart point having straight to convex sides, corner notches, and an expanded stem with deeply concave basal edges that may have a recurved appearance. Shoulders are barbed when the point is new; barbs are absent when the point has been resharpened several times. There is some resemblance to Fairland and Uvalde points found in the same general area.

Distribution: Frio points are found primarily in a large part of central Texas. The postulated dates for it indicate a Late Archaic through Woodland affiliation.

1.00-1.50

WEST OF MISSISSIPPI

GARY: 1000 B.C. to A.D. 1700

Description: This is a small to medium-size dart point and knife having straight, concave, or recurved edges on the blade, and a contracting stem. Shoulders are angular, stems are usually narrow and sometimes pointed. Similar points found elsewhere usually have names compatible with their area of provenence.

Distribution: The Gary point is found primarily in western Arkansas, northern Louisiana, northeastern Texas, eastern Oklahoma, southeastern Kansas, and southwestern Missouri, and are affiliated with Late Archaic Woodland, and Caddoan peoples in those states.

1.00-1.50

WEST OF MISSISSIPPI

GARZA: Earlier than A.D. 1500

Description: This is a triangular arrow point having a deep basal notch. Blade edges may be straight to convex or recurved. The basal notch may be U-shaped, V-shaped, or recurved. Blade edges are sometimes serrated. They are a variant of the Toyah points which have side-notches.

Distribution: Garza points are found in the northern portion of the state of Chihuahua, Mexico, and adjacent parts of Texas from El Paso County on the west to Lamb and Bailey counties on the east. Their cultural affiliation is not known at present.

1.00-1.50

WEST OF MISSISSIPPI

GLENDO: 1000 B.C. to 500 A.D.

Description: This is a small to medium size dart point having a thin, triangular shaped blade with convex edges, strongly barbed shoulders, basal edge convex to straight and a strongly expanding stem. Shows very good workmanship. Chipping is irregular.

Distribution: Found in the Northwest Plains area.

7.00-10.00

WEST OF MISSISSIPPI

GLENDO NOTCHED BASE: 1000 B.C. to 500 A.D.

Description: This small to medium size dart point has a thin, triangular blade with convex edges. Notches cut in at a 45 degree angle form the well barbed shoulders. The basal edge is convex and has a deep notch cut into the center. Stem is expanding. Flaking is irregular and the workmanship is very good.

Distribution: Found in the Northwest Plains area.

5.00-10.00

WEST OF MISSISSIPPI

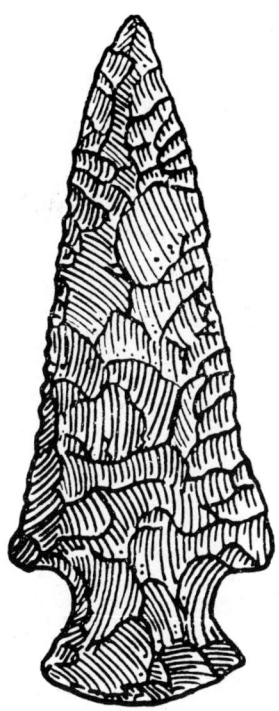

GODLEY: 500 B.C. to A.D. 500

Description: This is a small dart point having straight to convex sides and a wide, short corner-notch. Shoulders are angular to lightly barbed. The basal edge is convex, stems are short. Stem edges are sometimes smoothed by grinding. If only the stems are found they may appear to be from Table Rock points. However, the makers of the two points do not seem to have occupied the same territory.

Distribution: They are found from north-central Texas northward into southern and southeastern Oklahoma, and were made by Late Archaic peoples. The date shown above indicates that it may also have been made in the Woodland period.

1.00-1.50

WEST OF MISSISSIPPI

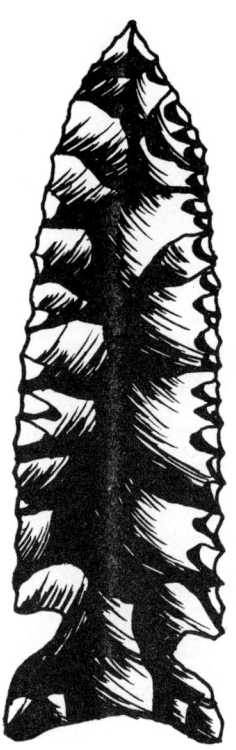

GRAHAM CAVE: 6000 to 5000 B.C.

Description: This is a long, narrow, lanceolate point having side-notches, and a deeply concave basal edge. Side edges may be straight to recurved, and serrated. Notches are wide and about as deep as they are wide. Basal corners droop and are usually pointed. Basal thinning extends to the notches. These points are similar to Osceola and Hemphill points but are earlier and have a deeper concave basal edge.

Distribution: They are found in Wisconsin, Illinois, Iowa, Missouri, western Arkansas, and eastern Oklahoma. They were made by Early Archaic peoples.

15.00-20.00

WEST OF MISSISSIPPI

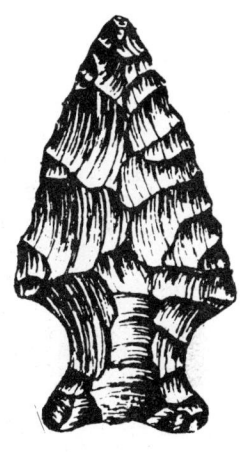

HANNA: 2500 to 850 B.C.

Description: This is a small dart point having convex sides and an expanded stem. The stem has a concave basal edge and rounded corners. Most stem edges are smoothed by grinding. Shoulders are angular to slightly barbed. Basal thinning may have resulted from forming the concave basal edge. Duncan and McKean points together with Hanna points, constitute a continuum for the type over a long time period.

Distribution: They are found in the Canadian Provinces of Alberta and Saskatchewan; in the Dakotas, Montana, Wyoming, Colorado, and peripheral areas on the Plains. A similar point is found in northeastern Oklahoma. They were made by peoples living in the Late Archaic period.

2.00-2.50

WEST OF MISSISSIPPI

HARRELL: A.D. 1000 to A.D. 1300

Description: This is a small, thin, triangular arrow point having three notches, one on each side of the stem, and one in the center of the basal edge. Side edges are usually straight, basal edges may be straight to slightly concave. Similar points are the Cahokia points of the upper Mississippi Valley, and Desert points found from Colorado and Wyoming to California.

Distribution: This point is found from northern Texas to Canada and is a product of Plains Indians prior to the introduction of the horse.

1.00-1.50

WEST OF MISSISSIPPI

HASKELL: A.D. 1200 to 1350

Description: This is a small, side-notched arrow point having straight to slightly convex sides, and a concave basal edge. Notches are close to the base entered diagonally so that the base has a curved appearance. Haskell points are related to Reed points found in the same area; the Reed points having a straight basal edge.

Distribution: It is found in western Arkansas and eastern Oklahoma primarily associated with Caddoan groups.

1.50-2.00

HAYES: A.D. 900 to 1200

Description: This is a small arrow point having recurved sides, barbs, and a "dovetail" shaped stem. Blade edges may be serrated, some have needle-like tips. They Hayes point is related to the Alba point which has a rounded or bulbous stem. They are found in the same areas.

Distribution: They are found in northern Louisiana, northeastern Texas, eastern Oklahoma, and western Arkansas, and were made by Caddoan peoples.

1.50-2.00

WEST OF MISSISSIPPI

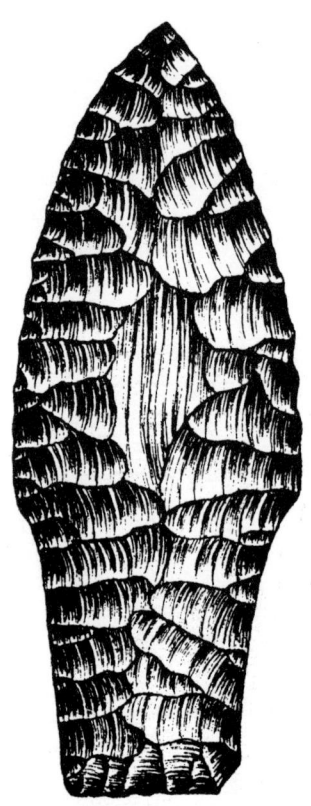

HELL GAP: 7500 to 6500 B.C.

Description: This is essentially a lanceolate point having a long, wide stem. Blade edges are convex, stem sections contract slightly, and basal edges may be straight to slightly concave or slightly convex. Basal edges are ground. This is probably a variant of the Agate Basin point. A similar point having a narrower stem is the Rio Grande point.

Distribution: They are found in Nebraska, Colorado, Wyoming, Idaho, the Dakotas, Montana, and southern Alberta in Canada, and were a product of early Archaic peoples.

8.00-9.00

WEST OF MISSISSIPPI

HOMAN: 800 to 1400 A.D.

Description: This small size bird arrowhead has a small, triangular shaped blade with slightly recurved edges. Edges are concave near the shoulders and convex near the tip. The point may be finely serrated and the stem is bulbous with a convex base. The shoulders vary from slight to strong with barbs.

Distribution: This point is found in the lower Mississippi Valley and East Texas.

1.00-3.00

WEST OF MISSISSIPPI

HOLLAND: 7500 to 6500 B.C.

Description: This is a large knife-like point having convex sides and a wide stem. Shoulders are usually very narrow, stems are straight to slightly expanded, and basal edges are straight to concave. Stem-edge smoothing is common to the type. They have a form similar to the Scottsbluff point but the Holland point is thinner. They belong in the Dalton cluster of points and have the same flint knapping techniques used in their manufacture.

Distribution: They are found in Wisconsin, Iowa, Illinois, Indiana, Missouri, Arkansas, and eastern Oklahoma, and were a product of early Archaic peoples.

6.00-6.75

WEST OF MISSISSIPPI

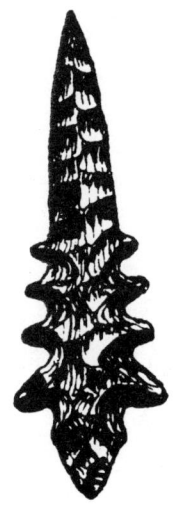

HOWARD: A.D. 1200 to 1300

Description: This is a small arrow point having 4 to 12 deep serrations on the edge of the blade accentuated by reducing the width of the tip to the base of the serrations. Stems are similar to those found on Alba or Hayes points. That is, they are rounded, bulbous, or diamond-shaped. They are related to Hayes and Alba points from the same area.

Distribution: They are found in northwestern Louisiana, northeastern Texas, southwestern Arkansas, and southeastern Oklahoma, and are a product of Caddoan Indians at the end of the Gibson period.

5.00-5.50

WEST OF MISSISSIPPI

HUFFAKER: A.D. 1000 to 1300

Description: This is a small, triangular arrow point having straight sides, a primary notch on each side near the base and sometimes one in the center of the basal edge, and a secondary notch, one on each side between the primary notch and the basal edge. Basal edges are straight. A variety of the Cahokia point is similar in size and form.

Distribution: It is found in western Arkansas, Oklahoma, Kansas, and other parts of the Plains, and were made by Plains Indians in late prehistoric times.

.75-2.00

WEST OF MISSISSIPPI

JOHNSON: 4000 to 3000 B.C.

Description: This is a medium to large point having convex sides and a straight to slightly expanding or contracting stem. The stem has a concave basal edge. Shoulders may be angular to barbed. Stem edges are sometimes smoothed. Appalachian points and Savannah River points in the eastern and southern states are similar in form but the Johnson point is older.

Distribution: They are found in southwestern Missouri, western Arkansas, eastern Oklahoma, and northeastern Texas, and were made by Middle Archaic peoples.

5.50-6.00

KEOTA: A.D. 1200 to 1350

Description: This is a small, ovoid arrow point having side-notches and a convex or fan-shaped stem. Notches usually enter horizontally from the sides, a few have been found where they enter at a slight angle. Keota points are made on a small Nodena-like point by the addition of notches near the basal end. It never seems to attain the length other Caddoan arrow points sometimes acquire.

Distribution: They are Caddoan points found in eastern Oklahoma, western Arkansas, and northeastern Texas.

.75-1.00

WEST OF MISSISSIPPI

LAKE MOHAVE: 7000 to 5000 B.C.

Description: This is a small to medium sIzed dart point having straight to very slightly concave or convex edges. The blade edges flare out for ⅓ length of blade then contract to well rounded base.

Distribution: Southern California.

.50-3.00

WEST OF MISSISSIPPI

LANGTRY: 1000 B.C. to A.D. 500

Description: This is a medium-size dart point having a contracting truncated stem and barbs. Side edges are usually straight to slightly concave or convex. Barbs are found on new specimens, but reduced to angular shoulders on resharpened points. Similar points found in the four corners area of Missouri, Kansas, Arkansas, and Oklahoma are of Middle Woodland age and known as Dickson points in the St. Louis area.

Distribution: They are found from central Texas southward into Mexico, and northward into southern Oklahoma, and were made by Late Archaic peoples.

1.00-1.50

WEST OF MISSISSIPPI

LIVERMORE: A.D. 700 to 1200

Description: This is an arrow point having a long, narrow blade, pronounced barbs extending horizontally, and a rectangular to slightly expanded, rounded stem. The shape is roughly cruciform in outline. Basal edges of the stem are generally irregular. It is a point type in the Livermore Focus.

Distribution: They are found in the area between Odessa and Van Horn, Texas, a dessert plateau.

1.00-1.50

WEST OF MISSISSIPPI

MCKEAN: 3000 to 2000 B.C.

Description: This is a lanceolate shaped blade with the sides incurved toward the tip and tapered toward the base. Occasionally there will be a point with just the reverse, rarely incurved toward both the tip and base. There is a deep symmetrical notch in the base with thin, sharp edges. The ears of the base are seldom of the same size or shape. This point is fairly rare.

Distribution: It is found over most of the Western United States.

2.00-5.00

WEST OF MISSISSIPPI

MESERVE: 7500 to 6500 B.C.

Description: This is a medium-size dart point or knife having straight to convex sides and a slightly convex basal edge. Side edges may be serrated and beveled on most specimens that have been resharpened several times. Stem edges are ground. The Meserve point is but one of many forms of the Dalton, its most distinctive feature being the slight basal concavity as compared to the deeper concavities on most other Dalton variants. Beveling is a common trait to most Dalton point forms.

Distribution: They are found in the Plains from Texas to Canada, and eastward to the Mississippi, and belong to the Early Archaic period.

7.00-10.00

WEST OF MISSISSIPPI

MILNESAND: 7500 to 6500 B.C.

Description: This is a medium-size lanceolate dart point having convex sides and a straight basal edge. The sides contract slightly towards the stem and are basally thinned. Basal edges are smoothed by grinding from ¼ to ⅓ of the length. This point is similar to the Plainview point, the difference being that the Milnesand point has a straight basal edge while the Plainview point has a concave basal edge. The Milnesand point also contracts towards the base, while the Plainview point maintains fairly straight sides.

Distribution: They are found in eastern New Mexico, western Oklahoma, and western Texas, and are Early Archaic points.

3.00-5.00

WEST OF MISSISSIPPI

MONTELL: 2000 B.C. to 1000 A.D.

Description: This is a medium to large size dart point having a triangular blade, edges which can be straight, concave, convex or recurved, and a short stem. The shoulders are more square than barbed and extend down in line with the base. The stem may be parallel, but usually expands and is split in the center by a deep notch. The base was strongly convex before the notch was removed. The Montell point is not very common.

Distribution: Found in central and western Texas.

2.50-4.00

WEST OF MISSISSIPPI

MORHISS: 2000 B.C. to 1000 A.D.

Description: This is a medium to large dart point. The blade is triangular with convex edges, small shoulders and a parallel stem that is very broad with a convex base. The barbs are small if present at all.

Distribution: The Morhiss point is found from the Rocky Mountains east.

1.00-5.00

WEST OF MISSISSIPPI

MORRIS: A.D. 900 to 1300

Description: This is a small, triangular arrow point having straight sides, side-notches, and a basal notch. Side edges may have fine serrations. The basal notch is usually a broad V-notch that gives the basal edge a recurved appearance. Basal corners are rounded. They have the same age and distributional range as the Keota points, so therefore may be related to them. The major difference would be the basal notch in the Morris point type.

Distribution: They are found in western Arkansas, eastern Oklahoma, southeastern Kansas, southwestern Missouri, and northeastern Texas, and were made by Caddoan peoples.

.75-1.00

WEST OF MISSISSIPPI

MOTLEY: 1300 to 500 B.C.

Description: This is a medium-size dart point having straight to convex sides, round, deep, corner-notches, and a narrow expanded stem. Barbs were created by the notching. Basal edges may be straight but most are slightly convex. Basal corners are often sharp, seldom rounded. The Motley point has a slight resemblance to the later Middle Woodland Snyders point farther north and may be ancestrally related.

Distribution: They are found in northeastern Louisiana, southeastern Arkansas, and northwestern Mississippi, and are a product of Late Archaic peoples affiliated with the Poverty Point Complex.

2.00-2.50

WEST OF MISSISSIPPI

NEBO HILL: 8000 to 5000 B.C.

Description: This is a medium to large size dart or spear point. Blade is lanceolate shaped with convex edges. The edges at the widest part tend to be parallel. The basal edge is straight to slightly concave or convex. The flaking is collateral or horizontal transverse, but may be random.

Distribution: The Nebo Hill point is found in the midwest United States.

15.00-20.00

WEST OF MISSISSIPPI

NODENA: A.D. 1400 to 1600

Description: This is a small, willow leaf-shaped arrow point having convex sides and a rounded base. A few points may have nearly pointed bases. They are widest near the center tapering to keen points. They are sometimes found in groups as burial offerings. One form is so narrow they look like small drills.

Distribution: They are found most often on Mississippian sites in northeastern Arkansas, southeastern Missouri, and western Tennessee. Near historic times, the Quapaw also made them while living on the lower Arkansas River.

1.00-1.50

WEST OF MISSISSIPPI

NORTH: 250 B.C. to A.D. 350

Description: This is a medium to large, broad, thin, ovoid to triangular point having convex sides and a convex basal edge. These points are found in groups with burials or buried in house floors. They are the basis for Snyders points.

Distribution: They are found on Middle Woodland sites in Ohio, Indiana, Illinois, Michigan, Wisconsin, Iowa, Missouri, eastern Kansas, and northeastern Oklahoma, associated with the Hopewell ceremonial and mortuary complex.

4.00-4.50

WEST OF MISSISSIPPI

OXBOW: 3500 to 3000 B.C.

Description: This is a small to medium-size dart point having convex sides and a distinctive base formed by the use of shallow side-notches and a concave basal edge. Basal corners are squared to rounded and have a drooping appearance. Basal thinning is noted on most points. They look similar to San Patrice points but have a later age.

Distribution: They are found from the Canadian Provinces of Saskatchewan and Alberta southward through the Dakotas, Montana, Wyoming, Colorado, and New Mexico, and were made in the middle to late Archaic period.

.50-.75

WEST OF MISSISSIPPI

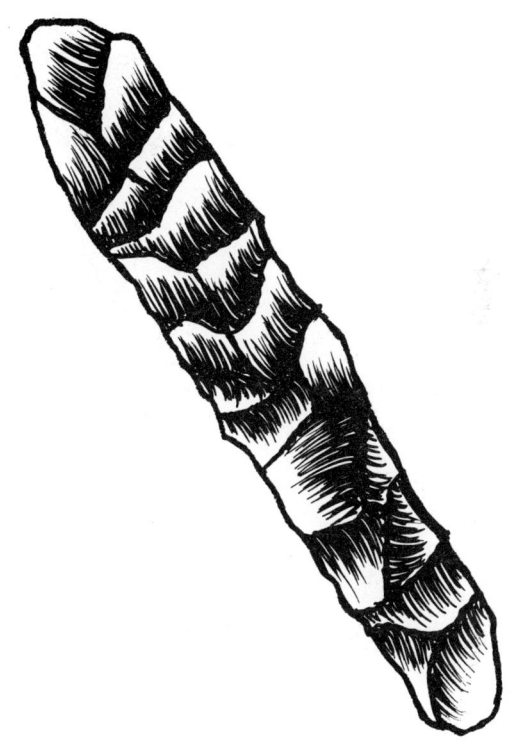

PANDALE: 2000 B.C. to 800 A.D.

Description: This small to medium dart point has a long, slender leaf-shaped blade with edges that are convex, straight or recurved to a needle tip. The stems vary from parallel to expanded or contracted and the shoulders are poor, often absent. The basal edge is straight, convex or concave. This type is most easily recognized by the beveling of the blade and the stem so strongly that it is like a propeller cross section. The Pandale point is rare.

Distribution: The Pandale point is found mostly in West Texas.

2.00-5.00

WEST OF MISSISSIPPI

PALMER: 6900 to 6500 B.C.

Description: This is a small dart point having a blade with straight to slightly convex sides, small corner-notches, and they may have serrated blade edges. Basal edges are straight and smoothed by grinding. Shoulders are barbed. They have approximately the same age and distributional range in which Kirk points are found.

Distribution: They are found from the Carolinas and Virginia westward in a narrow band ending in the southwestern Arkansas, southeastern Oklahoma, and northeastern Texas area.

2.00-2.50

WEST OF MISSISSIPPI

PAROWAN: A.D. 750 to 1000

Description: This is a triangular arrow point having straight sides and shallow basal notches. Notches may be inserted parallel to, or diagonally towards, the center of the blade. This is a highly localized point type having a distinctive form.

Distribution: They are found in southwestern Utah and parts of adjoining states, and are associated with the Southern Phase of the Fremont Culture.

2.00-2.50

WEST OF MISSISSIPPI

PEDERNALES: 4000 to 1000 B.C.

Description: This is a medium to large-size dart point having straight to slightly convex edges on the blade, and rectangular to slightly contracting bifurcated stem. Shoulders are prominent and angular. They are associated with late Archaic groups.

Distribution: They are found in a large part of Texas from the coastal, central, and north-central areas.

5.00-5.50

WEST OF MISSISSIPPI

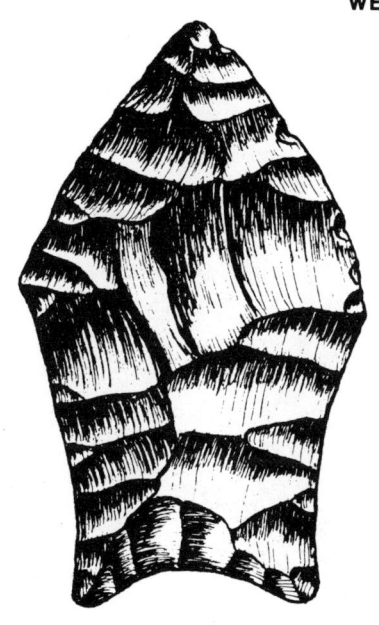

PELICAN: Late Paleo or Early Archaic

Description: This is a small dart point having a pentagonal-like form. Blade edges are straight to convex, stem edges are concave, and basal edges are moderately concave and ground. Basal thinning noted on the stems. This point has not been found in a datable context. Its attributes and places of discovery attest to their antiquity.

Distribution: They are found on old land surfaces in northwestern Louisiana, northeastern Texas, eastern and southwestern Arkansas, and southeastern Oklahoma.

9.00-10.00

WEST OF MISSISSIPPI

PELICAN LAKE: 300 to 150 B.C.

Description: This is a medium-size dart point having corner-notches. The blade may have straight to convex edges, notches are narrow, shoulders are barbed and sharp, and stems are expanded and may have straight to convex basal edges. Similar points are found in Wyoming, Colorado, Kansas, and northeastern Oklahoma.

Distribution: They are found from the Canadian Provinces of Saskatchewan and Alberta, southward into the northwestern Plains, and are a project of peoples living in the Early Woodland period.

2.00-2.50

WEST OF MISSISSIPPI

PERDIZ: A.D. 1000 to 1500

Description: This is a small arrow point having a triangular blade, prominent barbs, and a long narrow, contracting stem with a pointed or rounded end. Blade edges are usually straight but may sometimes be slightly convex or concave. It was made by Late Prehistoric peoples some of who were members of the Heneietta, Wylie, Frankston, Galveston Bay, and Rockport Foci.

Distribution: They are found in most of Texas and in south-central Oklahoma.

2.00-2.50

WEST OF MISSISSIPPI

PINTO BASIN: 1500 B.C. to 500 A.D.

Description: This is a small to medium size point having a short, triangular blade with straight to slightly convex or concave edges. The stem is about ⅓ the length of the entire blade and expands, has very weak shoulders with no barbs and a base that is convex to straight. A shallow notch has been taken from the center of the base.

Distribution: Found plentifully in California.

1.00-3.00

WEST OF MISSISSIPPI

PLAINVIEW: 7500 to 7000 B.C.

Description: This is a medium-size, lanceolate dart point usually having parallel sides and a concave basal edge. Flaking is quite uniform and of the parallel-transverse type. Basal thinning is common. Basal edges are ground. It has many similarities to Folsom points but may be slightly younger.

Distribution: They are found from Missouri, Arkansas, and Louisiana, westward to the Rockies, and from northeastern Mexico to Canada.

8.00-9.00

WEST OF MISSISSIPPI

Pogo: 250 B.C. to 1600 A.D.

Description: This is a large size dart point with a thick, triangular to leaf-shaped blade with concave to convex edges. The stem is usually parallel edged, but may be slightly contracting and has shoulders square to well barbed. The basal edge is straight to convex. Chipping broad random. This pont is not very plentiful.

Distribution: Found east of the Great Plains area.

3.00-5.00

WEST OF MISSISSIPPI

REED: A.D. 1000 to 1400

Description: This is a small, triangular, side-notched arrow point. Side and basal edges are straight, notches are low, creating a narrow base that may have squared or rounded ends. It differs from most side-notched arrow points in that the shoulders and edges of the base are about the same width.

Distribution: They are found in western Arkansas, eastern Oklahoma, southeastern Kansas, and southwestern Missouri, and were made by Caddoan or Caddo related peoples.

.75-1.00

WEST OF MISSISSIPPI

REFUGIO: 2000 to 1000 B.C.

Description: This is a medium to large-size ovoid dart point or knife. Refugio points are found in a variety of Late Archaic contexts and may have been used more as knives than projectile points.

Distribution: They are found in the mid-section of Texas from the coast to Oklahoma. Similar points have been found in southern and eastern Oklahoma and western Arkansas.

.75-1.00

WEST OF MISSISSIPPI

RICE: Early Archaic period.

Description: This is a medium to large-size dart point or knife having straight to slightly convex sides and an expanded, bifurcated base. Notches seem to originate high in the corners entering diagonally upward creating angular barbs. The basal edge is concavo and basal corners are lobed. Basal edges are smoothed by grinding. When resharpened several times, serrations and a pronounced bevel occur on the blade edges — features usually found on knives.

Distribution: They are found in the Ozark mountain areas of Missouri, Arkansas, and eastern Oklahoma.

1.00-1.50

WEST OF MISSISSIPPI

SAN PATRICE: Early Archaic period.

Description: This is a small dart point having straight to convex sides and a concave-sided stem. The basal edge is also concave. There are two varieties: Hope and St. John's. The Hope variety have a Dalton-like stem with broad concave side edges and the St. John's variety has shallow side-notches close to the basal edge. The St. John's variety has a remarkable resemblance to the Hardaway point.

Distribution: They are found in northern Louisiana, southeastern Oklahoma, southern and eastern Arkansas, northeastern Texas, and northwestern Mississippi.

2.00-2.50

WEST OF MISSISSIPPI

SANDIA: Paleo period.

Description: This is a medium-size dart point or knife having convex edges and a contracting stem. It is ovoid in form. There are two varieties, one has a rounded stem end and the other has a truncated stem. Notching occurs only on one side creating a shoulder and an offset stem. Stem edges are ground. Many contracting stemmed points of later date exist that have one shoulder, especially the Gary point. The form was altered when Indians resharpened them more often on one side. These are not Sandia points nor have any been certified found outside of New Mexico.

Distribution: They are found in a very limited area in New Mexico, primarily at Sandia Cave and at the Lucy Site.

20.00-22.00

WEST OF MISSISSIPPI

SCALLORN: A.D. 500 to 900

Description: This is an early, corner-notched arrow point having straight to convex blade edges, barbed shoulders, and an expanded stem. The basal edge is straight, rarely convex. The term Scallorn originally included a variety of Woodland and Caddoan corner-notched points, most of which have now been renamed leaving the Woodland variety to retain the designation Scallorn.

Distribution: They are found on Late Woodland sites in Texas, Oklahoma, Arkansas, and northern Louisiana.

1.50-2.00

WEST OF MISSISSIPPI

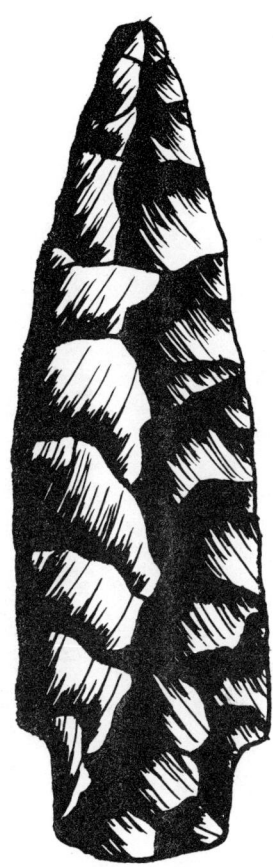

SCOTTSBLUFF: 7500 to 6000 B.C.

Description: This is a small to large, early point having parallel-sided to triangular blades, and a short, broad, rectangular stem. Shoulders are weakly defined, never barbed. Flaking may be random or of the parallel-transverse kind. Cross-sections are usually lenticular. It is an Early Archaic point.

Distribution: They are found from British Columbia, Saskatchewan, and Alberta in Canada, into Washington, Montana, the Dakotas, Wyoming, Colorado, Nebraska, New Mexico, Texas, northwestern Louisiana, southwestern Arkansas, and Oklahoma in the U.S. A few are scattered throughout Missouri.

10.00-11.00

WEST OF MISSISSIPPI

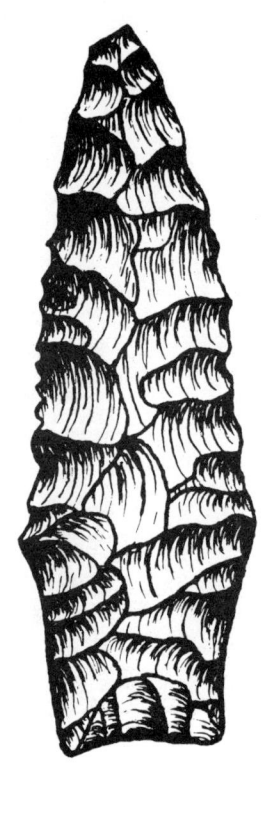

SEARCY: Middle Archaic period

Description: This is a medium-size, lanceolate point or knife having straight to slightly convex sides and a truncated, contracting stem. Blade edges may be serrated and beveled. The basal edge is concave, stem edges are ground. It seems to be a combination of the Dalton (blade) and the Agate Basin (stem) points.

Distribution: They are found in the Ozark Mountain areas of southern Missouri, Arkansas, and eastern Oklahoma.

10.00-11.00

WEST OF MISSISSIPPI

SEQUOYAH: A.D. 1000 to 1350

Description: This is a small, slender arrow point having straight serrated sides and an expanded stem. The basal edge is convex. This is a Caddoan and Mississippian arrow point.

Distribution: They are found in Missouri, Arkansas, and eastern Oklahoma, particularly with burials in the Spiro mounds.

1.50-2.00

WEST OF MISSISSIPPI

SHUMLA: 500 B.C. to 800 A.D.

Description: This point is small with a blade that is small & triangular. The edges may be straight, convex or concave. The barbs are short to long and may extend into line with base. Usually the base is straight to convex, rarely concave. The blade may be serrated.

Distribution: Found from the Rocky Mountains East.

1.00-3.00

WEST OF MISSISSIPPI

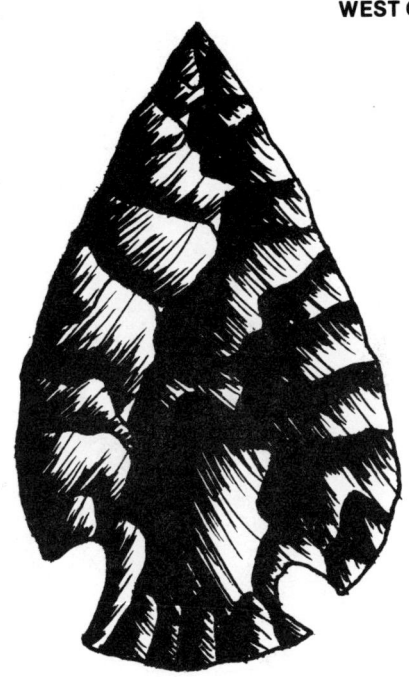

SNYDERS: 250 B.C. to A.D. 350

Description: This is a medium to large dart point. It is thin and wide, having convex sides, broad corner-notches, and an expanded stem. Snyders points are notched versions of North points. Glossy red, pink, cream, orange, and white points were made from heat treated chert.

Distribution: It is found in Ohio, Indiana, Illinois, Michigan, Wisconsin, Iowa, Missouri, eastern Kansas, and northeastern Oklahoma, and is associated with the Hopewell Ceremonial and Mortuary complex.

4.00-6.00

WEST OF MISSISSIPPI

STARR: 1600 to 1800 A.D.

Description: This is a small point with a triangular blade. The edges vary from slightly concave to strongly convex. Base is concave and often V-shaped. Fairly plentiful in certain restricted areas.

Distribution: Southern and central Texas.

1.00-2.50

WEST OF MISSISSIPPI

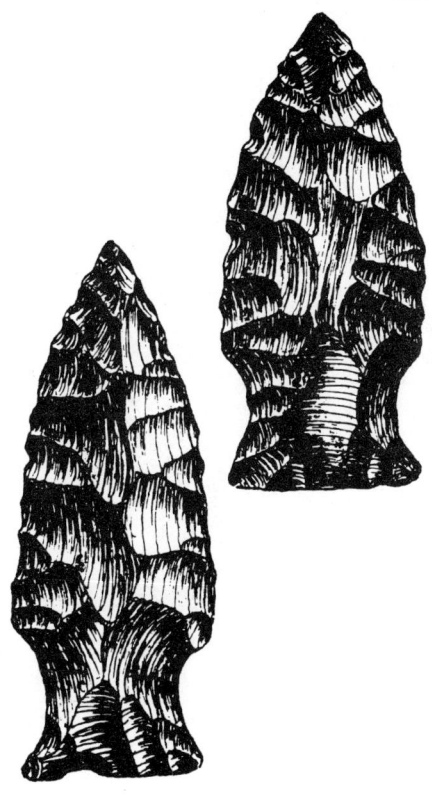

STEUBEN: A.D. 350 to 800

Description: This is a medium-size dart point having convex sides and an expanded stem. Shoulders are angular, never barbed. Basal edges are usually straight, some may be slightly ground. Similar points representing the same cultures but in different areas are: Lowe points (southern Illinois and Indiana), Bakers Creek points (Kentucky, Tennessee, and Alabama), and Chesser points (Ohio).

Distribution: They are found on Late Hopewell and Early Late Woodland sites in Illinois, Missouri, and Iowa.

2.00-2.50

WEST OF MISSISSIPPI

STILWELL: 7000 to 6000 B.C.

Description: This is a medium to large dart point or knife. It is long narrow, the blade having parallel sides that may be slightly convex or recurved. The edges may be serrated. Diagonal notches enter at or above the basal corners creating small, sharp barbs and an expanded stem. They have a remarkable resemblance to Kirk corner-notched points but are usually larger and better made. It is likely that they are related.

Distribution: They are found in Iowa, Wisconsin, Illinois, Missouri, Indiana and northeastern Arkansas, and are of Early Archaic age.

20.00-22.00

WEST OF MISSISSIPPI

TABLE ROCK: 1500 B.C.

Description: This is a small to medium-size dart point having convex sides, angular shoulders, and an expanded stem. Stem edges are usually heavily ground. Basal edges may be straight to slightly convex, rarely concave. Some collectors refer to these as "bottleneck" points.

Distribution: They are found in Wisconsin, Iowa, Michigan, Illinois, Ohio, Indiana, Missouri, Arkansas, eastern Kansas, and northeastern Oklahoma.

2.00-4.00

WEST OF MISSISSIPPI

TORTUGAS: 2000 B.C. to A.D. 500

Description: This is a small, triangular dart point having straight sides and a straight to slightly concave basal edge. Basal thinning is noted on most specimens. Edges may be beveled on resharpened points. It is likely these points served as knives as well as dart points.

Distribution: They are found in southern Texas and northeastern Mexico.

1.00-2.00

WEST OF MISSISSIPPI

TOYAH: Earlier than A.D. 1500

Description: This is a small, triangular arrow point having side-notches and a wide basal notch. The basal notch is usually recurved. Blade edges may be serrated. They are a variant of the Garza point having the addition of side-notches.

Distribution: They are found in the northern portion of the state of Chihuahua, Mexico, and adjacent parts of Texas from El Paso County on the west to Lamb and Bailey counties on the east. Their cultural affiliation is not known at present.

1.00-1.50

WEST OF MISSISSIPPI

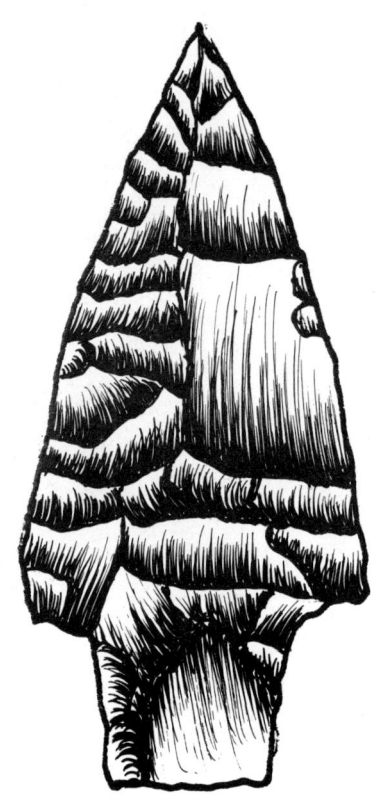

TRAVIS: 4000 B.C. to 1000 A.D.

Description: This is a medium size dart point with straight to convex edges. The blade is leaf-shaped with shoulders that are slight and rounded and a rectangular stem with parallel edges or may expand or contract slightly. Usually the basal edge is straight, but may be slightly convex or concave.

Distribution: Central Texas and surrounding areas.

1.00-3.00

WEST OF MISSISSIPPI

UVALDE: Late Archaic period

Description: This is a slender, medium-size dart point having broad corner-notches and an expanded stem. Shoulders are weak to slightly barbed and the basal edge is deeply concave. The basal corners are rounded. The type has not been dated but is expected to occur throughout most of the Late Archaic period.

Distribution: They are found in Texas, Oklahoma, northwestern Louisiana, and western Arkansas.

2.00-4.00

WEST OF MISSISSIPPI

WASHITA: A.D. 1100 to 1600

Description: This is a small, triangular arrow point having side-notches high on the basal end. Basal edges are straight, rarely concave. While it is similar to other side-notched points its major difference is the fact that the notches are farther up on the sides than the others.

Distribution: They are found in Oklahoma, northern Texas, New Mexico, and Kansas.

1.00-1.50

WEST OF MISSISSIPPI

WAUBESA: 500 B.C. to A.D. 500

Description: This is a medium-size point or knife having straight to convex sides and a broad contracting stem. Shoulders are angular, never barbed. They are a product of Early and Middle Woodland peoples. The Adena point may be related to it.

Distribution: They are found in Ohio, Indiana, Michigan, Wisconsin, Illinois, Iowa, Arkansas, northeastern Oklahoma, Kansas, Nebraska, and eastern Colorado.

4.00-4.50

WEST OF MISSISSIPPI

WELLS: Late Archaic period

Description: This is a medium-size dart point having a triangular blade and a long contracting stem. The basal end of the stem is usually rounded and edges are ground. Shoulders are weak, angular, and never barbed. This point is similar to the Morrill point found in much of the same areas, except the Morrill point has straight sides on the stem.

Distribution: They are found in central and northeastern Texas, Oklahoma, and southwestern Arkansas.

.50-.75

WEST OF MISSISSIPPI

WILLIAMS: 4000 to 1000 B.C.

Description: This is a medium-size dart point having convex sides, broad corner-notches, a convex basal edge, and an acute to needle-like point. The Big Creek point in northeastern Arkansas is almost similar but generally smaller.

Distribution: They are found in Texas, Oklahoma, Arkansas, Missouri, and Illinois.

3.50-5.50

EAST OF MISSISSIPPI

ADENA: 800 B.C. to A.D. 100.

Description: A fairly large point having convex side edges and a broad, contracting to rounded stem. Some examples have prominent shoulders. Some are well made and thin, and some have smoothed basal edges. The type is more commonly associated with Early and Middle Woodland peoples.

Distribution: They are found primarily in Ohio and the bordering states of Kentucky, Indiana, Pennsylvania, West Virginia, and Tennessee.

3.00-5.00

EAST OF MISSISSIPPI

APPALACHIAN: 4000 to 500 B.C.

Description: This is a large dart point having a flattened, triangular blade with convex edges that tend to be parallel near the stem. A broad stem that may be straight, slightly contracted or expanded and small shoulders that are usually tapered. Usually the stem area is ground and the base is concave. The point is often made of quartzite. Random chipping with some retouching and thinning on base.

Distribution: Found in the Mississippi Valley.

5.00-10.00

EAST OF MISSISSIPPI

ASHTABULA: 1500 to 500 B.C.

Description: This is a medium to large-size point having angular shoulders and an expanding stem. The stem necks down from broad shoulders to the stems basal corners in a steep graceful curve that helps to distinguish the type. Its large size, 2½ to six inches, indicates it was probably used more as a knife than a dart point.

Distribution: It is found in Ohio and parts of adjoining states and was made by Late Archaic or Early Woodland peoples.

3.00-3.50

EAST OF MISSISSIPPI

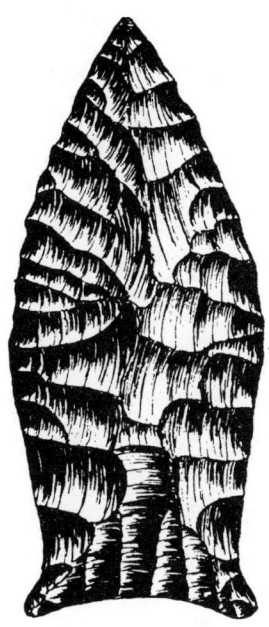

BEAVER LAKE: 8000 B.C.

Description: This is a medium-size dart point having recurved sides and an expanded base. Basal edges are thinned and concave. Stem edges are ground smooth for hafting. They have been referred to as unfluted Cumberland points but are smaller, wider, and thinner than the Cumberland type.

Distribution: These points are found in Alabama, Tennessee, Kentucky, northern Mississippi, southern Ohio, southern Indiana, and southern Illinois, and were made by late Paleo Indians.

20.00-22.00

EAST OF MISSISSIPPI

BENTON: 3500 to 1200 B.C.

Description: This is a medium to large spear point or knife with edges that tend to be straight, almost parallel. The blade is triangular with convex sides. The stem is straight or slightly incurved, broad and beveled on all edges. On the basal corners of the stem, there are tangs or ears. The basal edge is straight to concave. Thick blades are often beveled and thin blades often show oblique parallel chipping. The shoulders are small.

Distribution: This point is found in Tennessee and the Tennessee Valley.

5.00-10.00

EAST OF MISSISSIPPI

BENTON: 4000 to 2000 B.C.

Description: This is a medium to large dart point having a lanceolate shaped blade with convex edges and an acute point. The stem is short, broad and beveled on all edges with sides that are usually concave or straight. The shoulders are small and may be at right angles or tapered. Usually the base is straight, but may be concave or convex. The chipping pattern is broad, shallow and random with some retouching.

Distribution: Found from the Mississippi Valley East.

5.00-10.00

EAST OF MISSISSIPPI

BIG SANDY: 3500 to 1200 B.C.

Description: This is a medium-size dart point having convex sides and wide, shallow side-notches. The basal edge may be straight or concave. The base is usually the widest part of the point. It resembles, in shape and time, the Godar points of Illinois and the Raddatz points of Wisconsin.

Distribution: It is found in the western half of Kentucky and Tennessee, and northern Alabama, and was made by Late Archaic peoples.

2.50-3.00

EAST OF MISSISSIPPI

BIG SLOUGH: 5000 to 2000 B.C.

Description: This is a medium to large size dart point with a large, broad, triangular shaped blade with sides near the tip convex and near the shoulders concave. A long, broad stem with slightly concave or convex sides and barbed shoulders. The basal edge is convex, thin and usually ground. The flaking pattern is random, broad and shallow with occasionally collateral chipping. There is broad retouching with some fine chipping along the edges, especially on the stem.

Distribution: The Big Slough point is found east of the Mississippi Valley.

10.00-15.00

EAST OF MISSISSIPPI

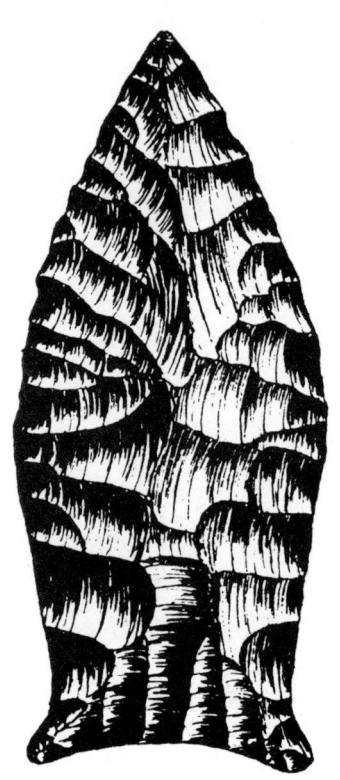

BEAVER LAKE: 8000 B.C.

Description: This is a medium-sized dart point having recurved sides and an expanded base. Basal edges are thinned and concave. Stem edges are ground smooth for hafting. They have been referred to as unfluted Cumberland points but are smaller, wider, and thinner than the Cumberland type.

Distribution: These points are found in Alabama, Tennessee, Kentucky, northern Mississippi, southern Ohio, southern Indiana, and southern Illinois, and were made by late Paleo Indians.

20.00-22.00

EAST OF MISSISSIPPI

BRADLEY: 2000 B.C. to 1 A.D.

Description: This is a small to medium sized dart point having convex to straight edges, stem edges concave to straight, and shoulders absent to very weak. The blade is narrow, thick, and triangular shaped. It is crudely made and shows little signs of retouching. The base is often unworked and can be convex, straight, or concave. Flaking is random and crude.

Distribution: East of the Mississippi Valley.

.50-2.50

EAST OF MISSISSIPPI

BREWERTON CORNER: 5000 to 2000 B.C.

Description: This is a medium size dart point having a broad, thick triangular blade with edges that are convex. The stem is expanding and has strong shoulders with small barbs. The basal edge will be convex, concave or straight and may be ground. The flaking is broad, shallow and random with some retouching.

Distribution: Found over most of the United States.

1.00-2.00

BREWERTON EARED: 400 to 1000 B.C.

Description: A small, 7/8 to 2 1/8 inch, to medium sized dart point having convex to straight edges and a thin, triangular blade with delicately chipped ears. The basal edge is concave, occasionally straight.

Distribution: Eastern and Central New York and Southern New England.

1.00-3.00

EAST OF MISSISSIPPI

CAHOKIA: A.D. 900 to A.D. 1400

Description: These are notched, triangular arrow points having straight sides with straight, concave or convex basal edges. They may have two primary side-notches, or two primary side-notches and one in the center of the base. Some have secondary notches on the base and sometimes on the edges of the blade. Some points are serrated on the side edges. These are probably the earliest notches triangular arrow points. Similar points in the Plains area are: Washita, Harrell, Reed, Huffacker, and Desert points.

Distribution: Cahokia points are found primarily at the Cahokia Site in west-central Illinois and at affiliated sites such as the one at Aztalan in Wisconsin. They are found in Missouri and at the Spiro site in Oklahoma.

1.00-1.50

EAST OF MISSISSIPPI

CATAHOULA: 1200 to 1600 A.D.

Description: This small bird point has a short, triangular blade with recurved or concave edges, a short, wide stem with a convex base and broad shoulders with distinctive barbs. The notches are narrow and form a broad barb. This point is scarce.

Distribution: Found in the Lower Mississippi Valley.

2.00-4.00

COPENA: A.D. 200 to 600

Description: This is a medium to large-size point having recurved side edges and a straight to slightly convex basal edge. A constriction occurs near the base to form an expanded stem. The Copena point is made by Middle to Late Woodland peoples who also made a point form that had straight to convex side edges.

Distribution: It is found primarily in the Tennessee River Valley in northern Alabama, in northern Mississippi and in most of Tennessee and Kentucky.

3.00-3.50

EAST OF MISSISSIPPI

COTACO CREEK: 500 B.C. to A.D. 300

Description: This is a broad, medium-size point having large rounded barbs and a short, straight stem. Blade edges may be straight or convex. The basal edge may be straight to convex. Stems are thinned, edges are ground. The point was made by Woodland Culture peoples.

Distribution: The distributional range is rather limited, the point occuring primarily on sites on the Tennessee River in northern Alabama and south central Tennessee.

1.50-2.00

EAST OF MISSISSIPPI

CUMBERLAND: 8000 to 6000 B.C.

Description: This is a medium to large, lanceolate, fluted point having recurved sides. A constriction near the basal end forms an expanded base that is eared. The basal edge is concave. Basal edges are ground. This is thought to be a late form of fluted point related to the Clovis point.

Distribution: Their center of distribution is in northern Alabama with lesser numbers found in southern Ohio, Kentucky, and Tennessee.

65.00-80.00

EAST OF MISSISSIPPI

DECATUR: 7500 to 6000 B.C.

Description: This is a small to medium-size point having convex sides when new, and straight to concave sides when used and resharpened. It has low corner notches, prominent barbs that flare outward, and a concave basal edge, the rim of which has been struck off. Some points are beveled and serrated. Basal edges are ground. This is an Early Archaic point most often used as a knife.

Distribution: They are found in southern Ohio, Indiana, and Illinois; northern Alabama and Georgia; western North Carolina; and in Kentucky.

2.50-3.00

EAST OF MISSISSIPPI

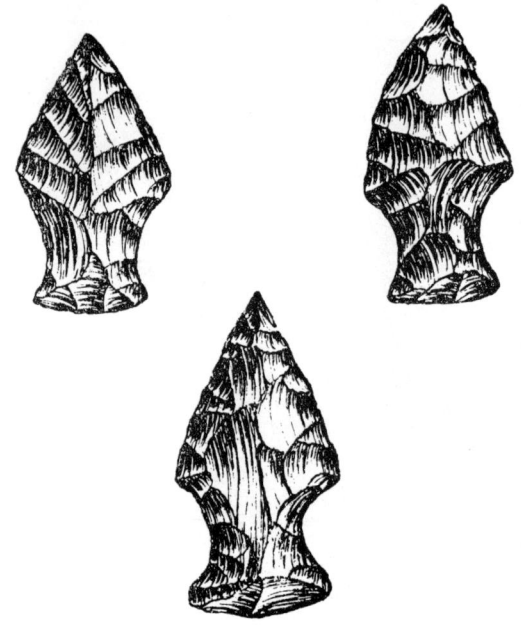

DURST: 1000 to 500 B.C.

Description: This is a small dart point with a broad notch and an expanded stem. Side-notches are broadly concave and two or three times wider than they are deep. Shoulders are angular. The edge of the blade and the basal edge are convex. These points have a resemblance to Table Rock points but are more crudely made. Table Rock points are earlier.

Distribution: They are found in a limited area of northern Illinois, Wisconsin, and western Michigan, and are a product of Late Archaic peoples.

.50-.75

EAST OF MISSISSIPPI

ECUSTA: 7000 to 5000 B.C.

Description: A small, triangular arrow point having beveled, straight sides, usually serrated. Near the base there are two shallow notches. The basal edges are usually straight, but may be concave or convex and thinned. This is a well made point.

Distribution: Southeast part of the United States.

2.00-3.00

EAST OF MISSISSIPPI

ELORA: 3000 to 1000 B.C.

Description: A medium to large size dart point with straight to nearly straight edges. The blade is thick, broad and triangular shaped with strong shoulders that taper into a tapering stem. A thick stem with straight to concave edges. The base is unfinished, being the broken edge of the original blank. Random chipping with fine retouching along the blade edges that results in fine serrations. This point is not too common.

Distribution: The Elora point is found from the Mississippi Valley East.

2.00-7.00

EAST OF MISSISSIPPI

EVA: 5000 to 3000 B.C.

Description: This is a medium to large dart point having straight to convex sides and shallow basal notches. The original preforms basal edge was straight. Notches are never deeper than they are wide. The type was named for the Eva Site in Benton County, Tennessee.

Distribution: These points are rarely found outside western Tennessee and represent a point type of the Middle Archaic period.

5.00-5.50

EAST OF MISSISSIPPI

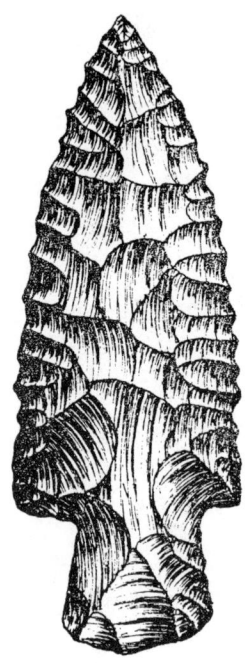

FLINT CREEK: 1000 to 200 B.C.

Description: This is a medium-size point having convex sides and a straight to slightly expanded stem. The stems basal edge may be straight to convex. Blade edges are often serrated. Shoulders are angular to slightly barbed. Flint Creek points have almost the same age and attributes as the Pontchartrain points found farther south and west indicating contemporaneity if not a relationship.

Distribution: They are found in southern Tennessee, northeastern Mississippi, and Alabama, on Late Archaic-Early Woodland sites.

2.00-2.50

EAST OF MISSISSIPPI

FLINT RIVER: 1 to 1200 A.D.

Description: This is a small to medium sized, narrow point with a lozenge shaped blade usually having convex edges or sometimes straight. Edges expand 2/3 of the way to the base, then contract to base. Usually the base is rounded, sometimes showing straight unfinished edges. A base that is thin is common for this type.

Distribution: Found mostly in the Mississippi Valley.

.50-1.50

EAST OF MISSISSIPPI

FORT ANCIENT: A.D. 1200 to 1600

Description: This is a long, slender, triangular arrow point having a straight to slightly convex basal edge. Edges may range from plain to strongly serrated. It is a point type of the Fort Ancient Culture — a Woodland people contemporary with Mississippi groups in the south and in the Mississippi Valley. Similar points are found on Mississippian sites such as Cahokia, where they are known as Madison points.

Distribution: It is found in southern Ohio and Indiana, and in northern Kentucky.

1.00-1.50

EAST OF MISSISSIPPI

FOX VALLEY: 8000 to 6000 B.C.

Description: This is a small dart point having straight, convex, or recurved edges on the blade, prominent flaring barbs, and a small, short, bifurcated stem with rounded basal corners. Some barbs curve so much that they appear to be reversed. A closely related point found in Ohio is known as the Erie point, differing from the Fox Valley point by having pointed basal corners.

Distribution: Fox Valley points are found in central and northern Illinois, southeastern Wisconsin, and northern Indiana, and are made by Early Archaic peoples who also made the larger Stilwell points.

1.00-1.50

EAST OF MISSISSIPPI

FRAZIER: 1200 B.C. to 100 A.D.

Description: This is a medium size lanceolate dart point with near parallel edges. The characteristics of the blade are flat and thin with the base additionally thinned and usually slightly incurved, but may be straight. This point is not too common.

Distribution: Southeast United States.

3.00-5.00

EAST OF MISSISSIPPI

FULTON TURKEY TAIL: 1000 B.C. to 500 A.D.

Description: This large size dart point has a flat, leaf shaped blade with both ends pointed, convex sides and notched near one end. Near the middle of the blade is the widest part. Usually the point is three times as long as wide, except on large examples. Chipping is broad, shallow and random with good retouching.

Distribution: Found from the Mississippi Valley east.

40.00-60.00

EAST OF MISSISSIPPI

GODAR: 2500 to 1500 B.C.

Description: This is a medium-size dart point having convex sides, acute tips, and wide side-notches. Side-notches are about as deep as they are wide. Basal edges are straight. Basal thinning extends to the notching. They are related to the Raddatz points found in Wisconsin but tend to be larger and better made farther south, probably because of the availability of better chert supplies.

Distribution: They are found in Illinois, eastern Missouri, western Indiana, and southern Wisconsin, and were made by Late Archaic peoples.

3.00-3.50

EAST OF MISSISSIPPI

GUILFORD: 6000 to 3000 B.C.

Description: This is a medium to large-size, lanceolate point having a contracting base with a concave basal edge. A few examples may have straight or convex basal edges. The basal edges on most specimens were smoothed by grinding up to one-third the length of the point. The apparent crude workmanship on these points was due more to the use of quartzitic and other difficult to chip materials rather than to the ability of the knapper.

Distribution: It is found in the Carolina Piedmont and in parts of adjoining states, and was made by Middle to Early Archaic peoples.

7.00-8.00

EAST OF MISSISSIPPI

HAMILTON: A.D. 300 to 800

Description: This is a triangular arrow point having convex sides and a straight to convex basal edge. A few points may have straight side edges; a few may be serrated. Controlled pressure flaking has produced a very well made point. Hamilton points may be among some of the earliest arrow points known in the United States.

Distribution: It is found primarily in eastern Tennessee and portions of nearby states. It is found in much of the Tennessee Valley, and was made by Woodland peoples.

3.00-4.00

EAST OF MISSISSIPPI

HARDAWAY: 8000 to 6000 B.C.

Description: This is a small, thin dart point having straight to convex sides, u-shaped side-notches close to the basal edge, and a recurved, concave basal edge. The Hardaway point is often found associated with other early Archaic points such as the Hardaway Dalton, Hardaway Blade, and Hardaway side-notched point. In its smaller form it closely resembles the St. John's variety of San Patrice point.

Distribution: It is found primarily in the Carolina Piedmont and probably occurs in adjoining areas. Its range has not been clearly established.

2.00-2.50

EAST OF MISSISSIPPI

HARDIN: 7500 to 6000 B.C.

Description: This is a small to large-size dart point and knife having straight to convex sides and a straight to expanded stem. Barbs are usually pronounced. Basal edges may be straight to concave, basal corners are sometimes lobed. Stem edges are smoothed by grinding. It is an eastern variant of the Scottsbluff point and consists of at least six varieties still unnamed.

Distribution: They are found in Ohio, Illinois, Indiana, Michigan, Wisconsin, Iowa, Missouri, Arkansas, Kentucky and Tennessee, and were made by Early Archaic peoples.

5.00-5.50

EAST OF MISSISSIPPI

HOPEWELLIAN: 700 to 1300 A.D.

Description: Sometimes called a basal notched Hopewellian. This is a large dart point having a large, oval blade that is thin and well chipped with convex sides. The basal edge is convex and notches cut in at an angle from the base. This point is rare.

Distribution: Found in the upper Mississippi and Ohio Valleys.

5.00-20.00

EAST OF MISSISSIPPI

HOPEWELLIAN: 700 to 1300 A.D.

Description: Sometimes called a dove-tail Hopewellian. This large dart or spear point has a narrow or leaf-shaped blade with a thin point and corner notches. The basal edge is concave. On large points the edges tend to be parallel. The flaking pattern is excellent.

Distribution: Found in the upper Mississippi and Ohio Valleys.

values to 65.00

EAST OF MISSISSIPPI

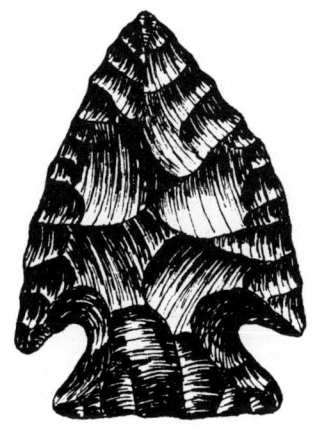

JACK'S REEF: A.D. 500 to 900

Description: This is a small dart point having convex or angular sides and an expanded stem. Notching is generally diagonal from the corners but some side-notched specimens occur. Barbs are small to medium in size. The basal edge is straight. They are a development from earlier Middle Woodland points varying primarily in having angular edges on the blades of some points.

Distribution: They are found in Ohio, New York, and Pennsylvania, and were made by Late Middle Woodland and Late Woodland peoples.

2.00-2.50

EAST OF MISSISSIPPI

KAYS: 3000 B.C.

Description: This is a medium to large dart point having a triangular shaped blade with edges from convex to straight. Usually the shoulders taper, but may be right angular. The stem is straight and slightly wider than long, having edges thinned and possibly ground. The basal edge is concave to convex. Random chipping, occasionally collateral, with short, regular secondary retouching. This point is fairly common.

Distribution: Found from the Mississippi Valley east.

3.00-8.00

EAST OF MISSISSIPPI

KIRK: 7000 to 6500 B.C.

Description: This is a medium-size dart point having straight, convex, or recurved edges, and deep serrations on the blade. The stem is short and rectangular, shoulders are angular to barbed. Often resharpened points may have alternate bevels on the blade. There are two basic varieties: Kirk stemmed and Kirk Corner-notched.

Distribution: Kirk points are found from West Virginia thru Virginia, the Carolinas, Georgia, Tennessee, and Kentucky. A variant form is found in southwestern Arkansas and southeastern Oklahoma.

3.00-4.00

EAST OF MISSISSIPPI

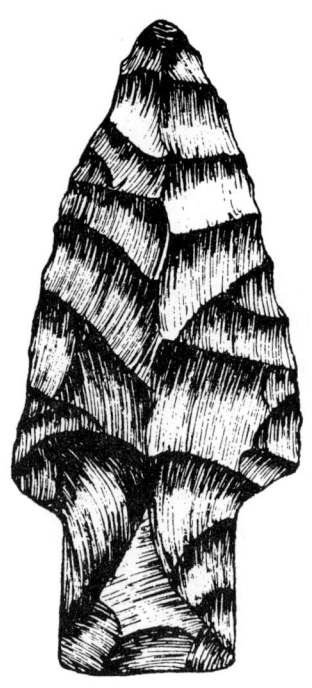

KRAMER: 1000 to 500 B.C.

Description: This is a medium-size dart point having convex edges and a medium-long rectangular stem. Shoulders are angular, basal edges on stems are usually straight, and corners are slightly rounded. Pronounced grinding on stem edges is common. Slightly earlier Archaic points have narrower stems and are barbed. Kramer points occur with Red Ochre burials and some of the earliest pottery made in the Mid-west.

Distribution: They are found in northeastern Missouri, southeastern Iowa, Illinois, Indiana, Ohio, and southern Wisconsin, and were made by Late Archaic-Early Woodland peoples.

2.00-2.50

EAST OF MISSISSIPPI

LECROY: 6500 to 6000 B.C.

Description: This is a small to medium-size dart point having serrated edges and expanded, deeply bifurcated stem. Basal edges are sometimes lightly smoothed by grinding. Lecroy points belong to a large group of early points having bifurcated stems such as the St. Albans, MacCorkle, and Kanawha points.

Distribution: Common in most eastern states from New York to Alabama, and westward to West Virginia, Ohio, Kentucky and Tennessee, and were made by Early Archaic peoples.

2.00-4.00

EAST OF MISSISSIPPI

LEVANNA: A.D. 700 to A.D. 900

Description: This is a small to medium-size, triangular arrow point having straight, concave, convex, or recurved sides and a straight to concave basal edge. Similar points found in the Carolinas are known as Yadkin points.

Distribution: They are found in southeastern Ontario and in the New England states, to as far south as the Carolinas, and were made by Late Woodland peoples.

1.00-1.50

EAST OF MISSISSIPPI

LOST LAKE: 7000 to 5000 B.C.

Description: This is a medium to large, corner-notched point or knife having straight, convex, or recurved sides and an expanded stem. Basal edges may be straight to convex. Basal grinding is noted on most specimens. Barbs are acute to rounded. Notches are usually curved. re-sharpened points usually have serrated, beveled edges. Lost Lake points have the same knapping techniques found on Thebes points, so it is likely the two are contemporaneous.

Distribution: They have been found in central and northern Alabama, central and eastern Tennessee and Kentucky, and southern Indiana and Ohio.

15.00-20.00

EAST OF MISSISSIPPI

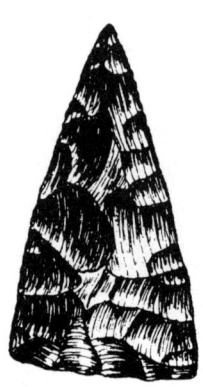

MADISON: A.D. 900 to 1750

Description: This is a thin, triangular arrow point having straight, concave, convex, or recurved sides, and a straight to slightly concave or convex basal edge. Some may have finely serrated sides. These were used almost exclusively in the unnotched form, in the later Mississippian period, but were the basis for the notched Cahokia points in the earlier Mississippian period.

Distribution: They are found on Upper and Middle Mississippi sites in Wisconsin, Iowa, Missouri, Illinois, and Indiana.

.50-.75

EAST OF MISSISSIPPI

MAPLES: 3000 to 1000 B.C.

Description: This is a large size dart or spear point having a large, thin, broad, triangular shaped blade with convex, occasionally straight sides. It has a short tapering stem with convex sides and a convex to straight base. The base is usually thinned and may be ground. Random flaking with very little retouching.

Distribution: This point is found from the Mississippi Valley East.

5.00-25.00

EAST OF MISSISSIPPI

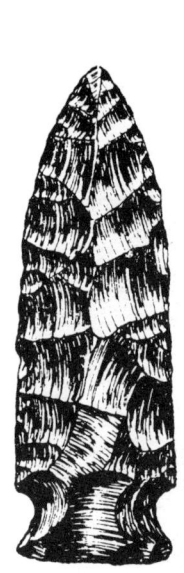

MATANZAS: 1500 to 1000 B.C.

Description: This is a small to medium-size dart point having acute tips, convex sides, wide, shallow side-notches near the basal corners, and straight to convex basal edges. The incidence of basal edge grinding is minimal. Broken points were often reworked into scrapers. It was erroneously renamed the Helton point during the Koster Site excavations in Illinois. In Ohio, a similar but serrated point is known as the Fish Spear point by collectors.

Distribution: They are found in Missouri, Iowa, Illinois, and along the Ohio River in southern Indiana and Ohio, and in northern Kentucky, and were made by Late Archaic peoples.

2.00-2.50

EAST OF MISSISSIPPI

MORROW MOUNTAIN: 5000 to 4000 B.C.

Description: This is a medium to large-size point having convex sides and a short contracting stem. The blade is often broad and triangular. Shoulders are wide and angular. Some have light grinding on the basal edges. The shape of these points is similar to the shape of preforms for most contracting stemmed points such as the Gary points and the Waubesa points.

Distribution: They are found in the Carolina Piedmont, in Georgia, Alabama, Tennessee, and Kentucky, and were made by Middle Archaic peoples.

1.00-2.00

EAST OF MISSISSIPPI

NATCHEZ: 500 B.C. to 500 A.D.

Description: This medium size dart point has a slender, triangular blade with straight to slightly convex or concave edges, prominent shoulders with no barbs and a base that is as wide or wider than the shoulders. The basal edge is concave.

Distribution: Found mostly in the Mississippi Valley.

2.50-15.00

EAST OF MISSISSIPPI

ORIENT: 1500 to 500 B.C.

Description: This is a small to medium-size dart point having a distinctive "fishtail" base. They have a narrow lanceolate form. The stem was formed with the introduction of broad, shallow side-notches which created an expanded stem and rounded shoulders. Basal edges are slightly concave. They are made from local quartzes, slate, and materials considered difficult to knapp.

Distribution: They are found in New York and surrounding states to the south, and are a project of the Late Archaic-Early Woodland transitional period.

1.00-1.50

EAST OF MISSISSIPPI

PEE DEE: A.D. 1500 to 1700

Description: This is a small, thin point having a pentagonal form. The base is rectangular to slightly contracting. Basal edges may be straight to slightly concave. A triangular arrow point named the Pee Dee Triangular point is associated with it.

Distribution: They are found in Georgia, in the Carolinas, and in Virginia, and are associated with the Proto-historic occupation of the area.

.75-1.00

EAST OF MISSISSIPPI

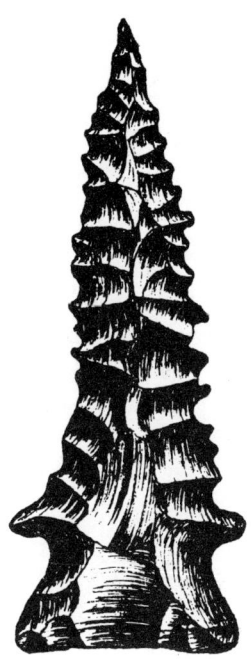

PINE TREE: 7900 to 6500 B.C.

Description: This is a medium-size corner-notched point having straight, convex, or recurved edges, prominent barbs, narrow diagonal notches, and an expanded stem. The stem may have a straight to convex basal edge. Basal edges are usually ground, blade edges are often serrated. A similar point found at considerable depth in West Virginia has been named the Charleston point.

Distribution: They are found in Georgia, Alabama, Tennessee, Kentucky, southern Indiana, and southern Ohio, and were made by Early Archaic peoples.

5.00-5.50

EAST OF MISSISSIPPI

PLEVNA: 5000 B.C. to 500 A.D.

Description: This medium to large dart point has a lanceolate to triangular shaped blade with straight, convex or concave edges. Corner notches, which are well made, set off the stem area which is not as wide as the blade and has a convex to semi-circle base which is thinned. The sides of the stem may be almost straight. Chipping is shallow, broad and random with bevel along one edge of each face produced by retouching. The shoulders are the widest part of the blade.

Distribution: From the Mississippi Valley east.

10.00-20.00

EAST OF MISSISSIPPI

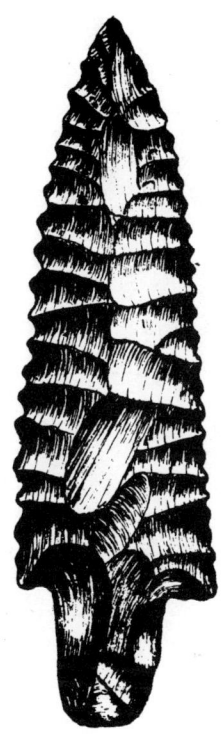

PONTCHARTRAIN: 1300 to 800 B.C.

Description: This is a medium-size point having straight, convex, or recurved edges, angular to lightly barbed shoulders, and a rectangular to slightly contracting stem. Basal edges usually have rounded corners. Flint Creek points are similar, have abut the same age, and may represent the type of the Tennessee Valley. Flint Creek points are different in that they sometimes have expanding stems.

Distribution: They are found on Early Woodland sites in the lower Mississippi Valley.

4.00-4.50

EAST OF MISSISSIPPI

QUAD: 8000 to 6000 B.C.

Description: This is a medium-size, lanceolate dart point having an expanded base with "eared" basal corners. The base is usually the widest part of the point. Side edges are recurved, basal edges are ground. Basal thinning is common and was used in lieu of fluting. The Quad point resembles the Cumberland point but is wider, thinner, and lacks the fluting.

Distribution: It is found in Alabama, Tennessee, Kentucky, Mississippi, and southern Illinois. Several have been found in northeastern Arkansas.

10.00-15.00

EAST OF MISSISSIPPI

RANDOLPH: A.D. 1700 to 1800

Description: This is a narrow, thick arrow point having a short, rectangular to contracting stem. Side edges may be straight to parallel convex. Flaking is large and irregular. Cross-sections may be diamond-shaped to lenticular. It is thought that these points were made by destitute bands of Indians in the historic period who had to rely on the bow and arrow again for hunting.

Distribution: They are found in North Carolina, eastern Tennessee, and the adjoining parts of South Carolina and Virginia.

.75-1.00

EAST OF MISSISSIPPI

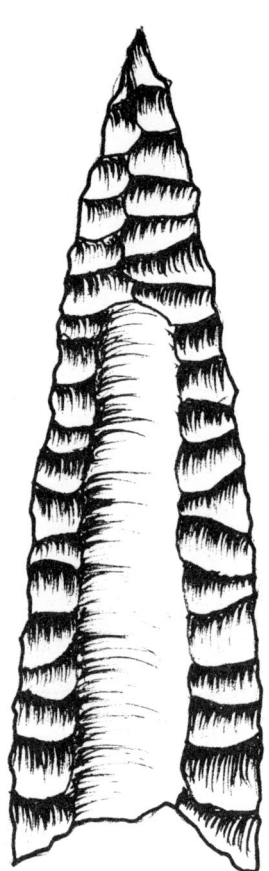

REDSTONE: 15,000 B.C.

Description: This is a large, triangular shaped blade having straight to convex sides and a concave to U shaped basal edge. The sides are parallel or near parallel near the base. Extending from the base is a flute, varying from short to almost full length of the blade. The flaking may be random or collateral.

Distribution: The Redstone point is found in southeastern United States.

values to 100.00

EAST OF MISSISSIPPI

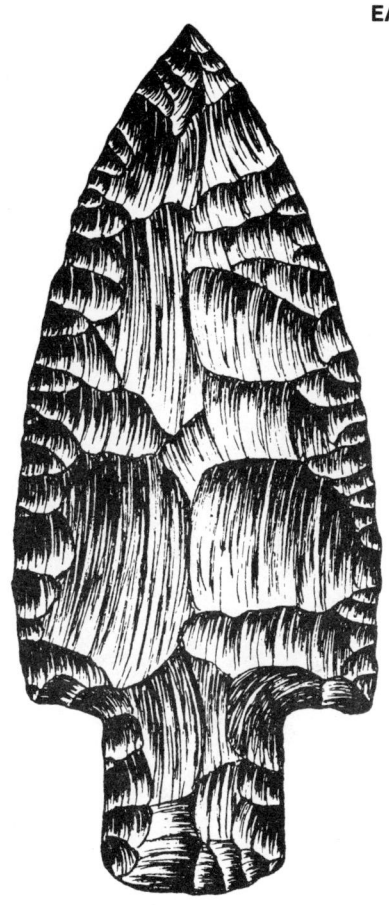

ROBBINS: 0 to A.D. 350

Description: This is a medium to large dart point having a broad, thin blade with convex sides and a rectangular stem. The stem has rounded corners. Shoulders may be angular to barbed. These points are often found made of colorful Flint Ridge flint and found in burial caches.

Distribution: They are found in Ohio, Indiana, Kentucky, West Virginia, and southwestern Pennsylvania, and were made by Late Adena peoples.

4.00-4.50

EAST OF MISSISSIPPI

ROSEVILLE: 3000 to 1000 B.C.

Description: A medium sized dart point that is thick with a lozenge shaped blade. The edges are straight to slightly concave.

Distribution: Found in the Chesapeake Bay Area north and east.

.50-1.50

EAST OF MISSISSIPPI

ROWAN: 7500 to 6500 B.C.

Description: This is a medium-size, side-notched dart point having convex sides, broad, shallow side-notches, and a concave basal edge. Basal corners are usually lobed or rounded and stem edges are ground. Basal thinning is common for the type. They may be related to the Dalton complex in which some points have broad side-notches and lobed or "eared" corners.

Distribution: They are found in North Carolina, South Carolina, Virginia, Georgia, and northern Florida.

2.00-2.50

EAST OF MISSISSIPPI

SAVANNAH RIVER: 3000 to 1000 B.C.

Description: This is a medium to large dart point with the edges convex possibly and parallel for the lower one-half of the point. The blade is triangular shaped and the stem is straight or contracting with sides concave or straight. Usually the shoulders are tapered, but may be right angular. The basal edge is usually thinned and is straight or concave. The flaking pattern is broad, shallow and random with some retouching on all edges. The usual size of this point is 2¼ to 6¼ inches and is not too plentiful.

Distribution: Found from the Mississippi Valley east.

5.00-25.00

EAST OF MISSISSIPPI

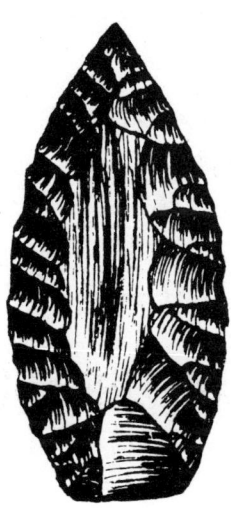

SHETLEY: A.D. 1300 to 1650

Description: This is a small arrow point having convex sides and a straight to slightly concave basal edge. Their widest point is below center and a few may be widest above center. It is a Late Prehistoric and Proto-historic point.

Distribution: It is found from Alabama to southern Illinois and western Kentucky, then westward to northwestern Arkansas and Oklahoma.

.75-1.00

EAST OF MISSISSIPPI

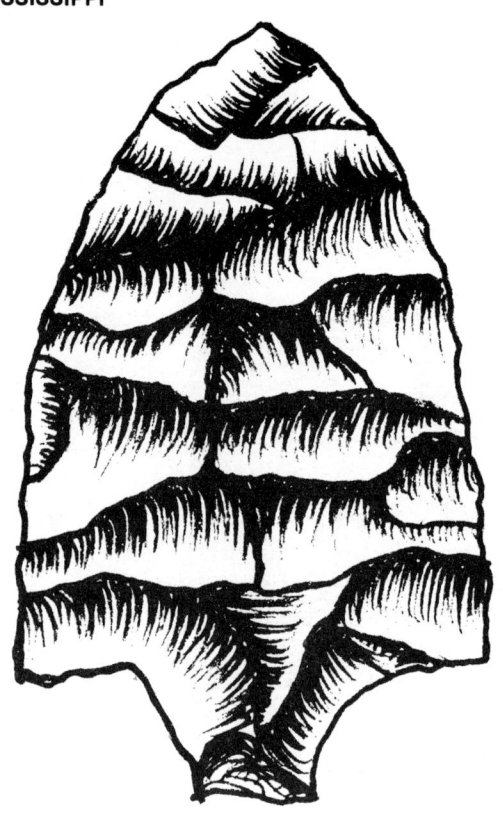

SNOOK KILL: 4000 to 1500 B.C.

Description: This is a medium to large size dart or spear point having a broad, thick triangular shaped blade with straight to convex sides, occasionally recurved near the shoulders. The shoulders are strong, but not barbed. The stem is short, thick and occasionally straight. Base is straight to slightly convex or concave. Random flaking with some retouching.

Distribution: Mississippi Valley east.

1.00-8.00

EAST OF MISSISSIPPI

ST. CHARLES: Early Archaic

Description: This is a small to large, corner-notched dart point or knife having convex sides and a convex basal edge. Notches are narrow, the stem is fan-shaped and has heavily ground edges. When resharpened the blade edges often acquire pronounced bevels. They are known as Dovetail points by collectors and may consist of several subtypes having stems that range from almost rectangular, to oval, to convex, but having a recurved basal edge.

Distribution: They are found in Pennsylvania, West Virginia, Kentucky, Tennessee, Alabama, Michigan, Wisconsin, Iowa, Illinois, Missouri, and Arkansas.

10.00-20.00

EAST OF MISSISSIPPI

STANLY: Middle Archaic period.

Description: This is a broad, triangular dart point having a small, squared, bifurcated stem. Shoulders are broad, barbed, and rounded. Some have serrations and beveled edges. Many of the points are made from hard to knapp materials such as rhyolite, andesite, quartz, and argillite.

Distribution: They are found in North Carolina, Tennessee, Kentucky, and parts of adjacent states.

2.00-2.50

EAST OF MISSISSIPPI

STEUBENVILLE: 5000 to 1000 B.C.

Description: These are medium to large size, lanceolate dart points with the widest part ⅔ of the distance from the tip to the base. Most have concave base, but may be almost straight and thinned. The sides are convex on the tip end and straight to convex on base end.

Distribution: Upper Ohio Valley to the Hudson River.

1.00-5.00

EAST OF MISSISSIPPI

STEUBENVILLE: 5000 to 2000 B.C.

Description: This is a medium to large dart point having convex edges and a concave to straight basal edge. The blade is broad and triangular with small, weak shoulders and a broad stem. Stem edges are straight or nearly straight. Random chipping with some retouching.

Distribution: Found from the Mississippi Valley East.

1.00-10.00

EAST OF MISSISSIPPI

THEBES: 7500 to 600 B.C.

Description: This is a medium to large dart point or knife having straight to convex sides, broad diagonal notches squared at the inner end, and a broadly expanded stem. Stem edges may be straight, concave, or slightly convex. Most have heavily ground basal edges. Two variants are known in Ohio and in Indiana: One has an upward curve to the notches; the other is side-notched — the notch expanding internally. These are called E-notched points by collectors.

Distribution: They are found in Ohio, Indiana, Illinois, Kentucky, Michigan, Wisconsin, Iowa, and Missouri.

15.00-16.00

EAST OF MISSISSIPPI

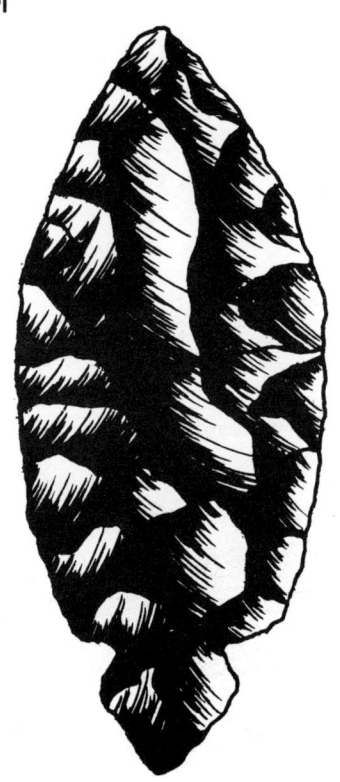

TURKEY TAIL: 1500 to 800 B.C.

Description: This is a very distinctive point. It is large, bi-pointed, has convex to recurved sides, and shallow notches near the base. It is very thin and usually well made. It is a product of Transitional Late Archaic-Early Woodland peoples.

Distribution: They are found in Michigan, Ohio, Indiana, Illinois, Wisconsin, eastern Missouri, and Kentucky.

35.00-45.00

EAST OF MISSISSIPPI

WHEELER: Early Archaic Period

Description: This is a medium-size, lanceolate dart point having convex sides and a deeply indented basal edge. Its widest point is near the base. The basal edge is thick and rarely thinned. It is similar to the McKean point found in the West, but is wider, thicker, and older.

Distribution: They are found from North Carolina westward through Alabama. The type is rare and the distribution is not well known.

8.00-10.00

EAST OF MISSISSIPPI

YADKIN: A.D. 600 to 1200

Description: This is a medium to large, triangular arrow point having a concave basal edge. Side edges may be straight, concave, convex, or recurved. A variant may have an almost imperceptible stem created by reducing the sides near the base. This point is probably the same as the Levanna point found farther north.

Distribution: They are found in Georgia, the Carolinas, and Virginia.

2.00-2.50

NATIONWIDE

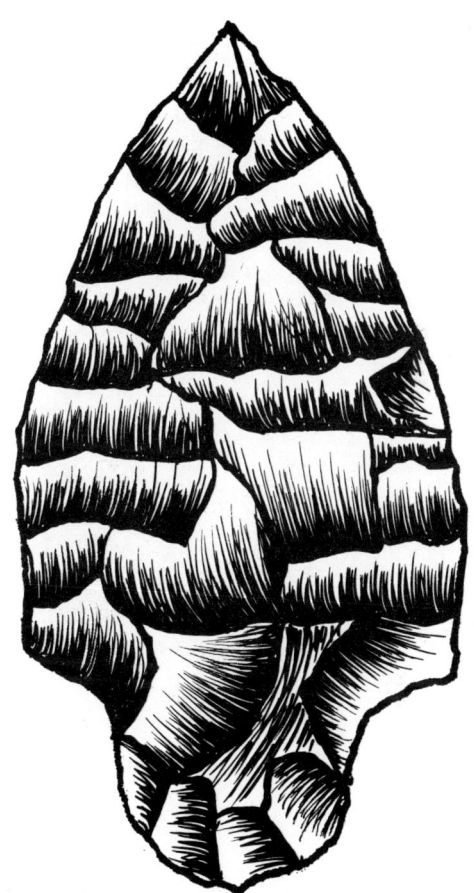

ADENA: 800 B.C. to 800 A.D.

Description: This medium to large sized dart point has a thin, triangular to lanceolate shaped blade with sides that are convex & almost straight near the shoulders. A long, rounded stem that may have straight sides and be slightly expanding, shoulders that are right angular to tapered, and a convex base are characteristics of this point. There is broad, random chipping that approaches collateral with fine retouching.

Distribution: Found over most of the United States.

5.00-15.00

NATIONWIDE

BAKER CREEK: 1500 B.C. to 200 A.D.

Description: This medium size dart point has a triangular shaped blade with straight to convex edges. The stem is one-third the length of the point and expanding with sides that are straight. It has small shoulders and vary from right angular to tapered. Usually the base is straight, sometimes convex, thinned, and lightly ground. The chipping pattern is broad, random with all areas retouched.

Distribution: Found over most of the United States.

1.00-5.00

NATIONWIDE

BARE ISLAND: 7000 to 3000 B.C.

Description: This is a medium to large dart point. The blade is narrow and triangular shaped with a pointed tip, straight to convex edges and rounded shoulders. The stem edges are straight and parallel and the base is straight to convex. The flaking is finely chipped and random.

Distribution: Found over most of the United States.

2.00-15.00

NATIONWIDE

BIG SANDY: 6000 to 1000 B.C.

Description: This is a small to medium size dart point having a thin, flat, triangular shaped blade with edges that are convex, side notches forming the shoulders, and a stem not as wide as the blade. The base is thinned and usually concave, occasionally straight. Usually there is random chipping with fine retouching, rarely may be oblique parallel chipping.

Distribution: Found over most of the United States.

2.00-7.00

NATIONWIDE

BROWN VALLEY: 8000 to 3000 B.C.

Description: This is a medium to large, broad lanceolate shaped blade having convex sides and a concave base. The base has been thinned to resemble short flutes. It may be ground. The flaking is fine, often horizontal or oblique transverse.

Distribution: This point is found over most of the United States.

10.00-25.00

NATIONWIDE

CLOVIS: 12,000 to 10,000 B.C.

Description: This is a fluted, lanceolate point ranging from 1½ to 8 inches in length. Side edges may be straight to slightly convex converging to a keen point. The basal edge is concave, rarely recurved. Flutes are ½ inch long or longer. Most have basal edge grinding. There are at least a half dozen distinctive forms of these points, some of which bear separate type names such as the Holcomb point.

Distribution: They are said to be found in all of the continental states, Mexico, and Canada, and were made by Paleo Indians noted for making the earliest stone points.

40.00-60.00

NATIONWIDE

COOSA NOTCHED: 500 B.C. to 500 A.D.

Description: This is a small sized dart point having a triangular blade with straight to convex finely serrated edges, shallow side notches, and the stem nearly as wide as the blade. Usually the base is thinned and is convex to concave. The edges of the blade may be beveled on one or both sides of each face. A cross-section shows the point is flat on one side and convex on the other. Chipping pattern is random.

Distribution: Found over most of the United States.

1.00-3.00

NATIONWIDE

CUNEY: 1600 to 1800 A.D.

Description: This is a small point having a triangular blade with edges straight or concave. Stem is paralled-edged or expanding with long, flaring barbs. The basal edge is concave to deeply U notched. This point is fairly plentiful.

Distribution: Found over most of the United States.

1.00-2.00

NATIONWIDE

DAMRON: 5000 to 2000 B.C.

Description: This medium sized dart point has a triangular shaped blade with straight or convex edges which may be finely serrated. The stem is as wide or nearly as wide as the blade. Usually the base and side notches is beveled and convex or straight. Chipping is deep, random with fine retouching.

Distribution: Found over all of the United States.

1.00-5.00

NATIONWIDE

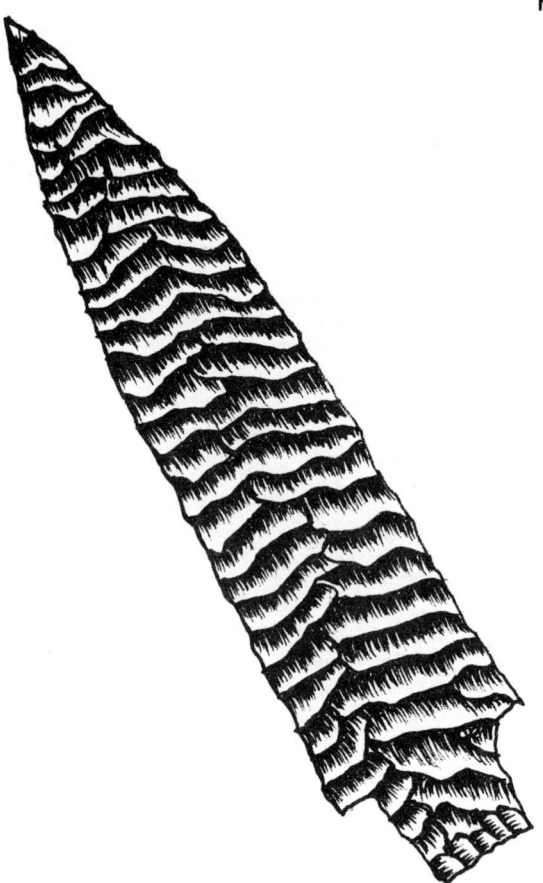

ELK RIVER: 4000 to 1000 B.C.

Description: This large dart point has a narrow, triangular shaped blade with convex edges. The stem is straight to expanded with the edges straight and the shoulders tapered and lightly barbed. The base is straight to slightly convex and sometimes lightly ground. Oblique-transverse chipping with very little retouching. Often there is a median ridge. The Elk River point is rare.

Distribution: Found over most of the United States.

2.50-20.00

NATIONWIDE

ELLIS: 1000 B.C. to 1000 A.D.

Description: This is a small to medium dart point having a short, triangular blade with straight to convex edges that are sometimes slightly concave. The stem expands toward the base, but is never as broad as the shoulders. Prominent shoulders that are well barbed and a straight to convex base are characteristic of this point.

Distribution: Found over most of the United States.

1.00-2.00

NATIONWIDE

GUNTERSVILLE: 1300 to 1800 A.D.

Description: This is a small to medium sized bird point with a lanceolate shaped blade. The edges are convex and the base is straight or nearly straight. The widest part of the point is at or near the base. Chipping is broad, random and shallow on the face with fine, secondary flakes at the edges.

Distribution: Found over a wide area of the United States.

.50-2.00

NATIONWIDE

HALIFAX: 2500 to 500 B.C.

Description: This small to medium dart point has a triangular shaped blade with sides that are straight to convex. The stem is expanding with concave or straight sides and small, tapered shoulders. The base is straight to convex and the edges are usually ground as are the stem edges. There is broad, random chipping with good retouching.

Distribution: Found over most of the United States.

.50-2.50

NATIONWIDE

HAMILTON: A.D. 300 to 800

Description: This is a triangular arrow point having convex sides and a straight to convex basal edge. A few points may have straight side edges; a few may be serrated. Controlled pressure flaking has produced a very well made point. Hamilton points may be among some of the earliest arrow points known in the United States.

Distribution: Found over most of the United States.

3.00-4.00

NATIONWIDE

JAKIE SHELTER: 5000 B.C.

Description: This small to medium sized dart point has a flat, triangular blade with convex edges, side notches forming the shoulders and a stem as wide as the blade. On the shoulders, thinning often runs from one notch to the other. One edge on each face of the point is often beveled. The basal edge is concave and thinned. Chipping is broad, shallow, random, often approaching horizontal transverse.

Distribution: Found over all of the United States.

1.00-8.00

NATIONWIDE

JUDE: 7000 to 4000 B.C.

Description: This is a small dart point having a triangular shaped blade with straight edges. The stem is straight, occasionally slightly expanding with shoulders usually right angular sometimes tapered or barbed. Stem is wider than it is long and the edges are straight. Usually the base is slightly ground and is concave or straight and thinned. Chipping pattern is broad, shallow and random with shorter retouching.

Distribution: Found over most of the United States.

1.00-3.00

NATIONWIDE

KNIGHT ISLAND: 1 to 1000 A.D.

Description: This medium sized dart point has a thin, lanceolate shaped blade with edges that are convex and tend to be parallel on some points. Usually the stem is not quite as wide as the blade. Side notches form the shoulders. The base is slightly concave or straight, thinned and lightly ground. Chipping is broad, shallow, random with fine retouching.

Distribution: Found over all of the United States.

1.00-5.00

NATIONWIDE

LAMOKA: 3500 to 500 B.C.

Description: This is a small size dart point. The blade is small, narrow and triangle shaped with straight to slightly convex sides, small and tapering shoulders and a straight to expanding stem. The basal edge is straight to slightly concave or convex. Often the base is as thick as the blade and exhibits an unmodified surface of the original flake. Random chipping with no retouching and the general appearance is of an unfinished point.

Distribution: Found over most of the United States.

.50-3.00

NATIONWIDE

LERMA: 2000 B.C. to 200 A.D.

Description: This is a medium size leaf shaped dart having a slender, double pointed, leaf shaped blade. Sometimes one end of the blade is more rounded than pointed. Blade edges are thick and steep and are thinned down enough at one end to haft. Crude chipping.

Distribution: Found over most of the United States.

1.00-7.00

NATIONWIDE

MARCOS: 2000 B.C. to 1000 A.D.

Description: This medium to large dart point has a triangular blade with straight, slightly recurved edges, strongly expanding stem and a straight to convex basal edge. Deep notches cut into the corners at about 45 degrees giving strong barbs, which extend in line with the base. The base is not as wide as the barbs.

Distribution: Found over most of the United States.

1.00-10.00

NATIONWIDE

MARSHALL: 500 B.C. to 1300 A.D.

Description: This is a medium dart point with edges usually straight to concave, rarely convex. The blade is thin, triangular and finely chipped. The shoulders are prominent to widely outflaring with barbs that may sweep outward. A long stem, contracting sometimes nearly parallel or even slightly expanding and a basal edge that is straight or concave, rarely convex are characteristics of this point. It is fairly plentiful.

Distribution: Found over most of the United States.

1.00-8.00

NATIONWIDE

MARTINDALE: 3000 B.C. to 1000 A.D.

Description: This small to medium size dart point has a triangular blade with convex or straight eges. The stem varies from nearly parallel to strongly expanding and has pronounced to well barbed shoulders. The basal edge resembles a "fish tail." It is formed by two convex curves meeting in a depression in the center. The Martindale pont is rare.

Distribution: Found over most of the United States.

1.00-5.00

NATIONWIDE

MOUNTAIN FORK: 3500 B.C. to 1 A.D.

Description: This small dart point has a narrow, thick, triangular shaped blade with edges that are straight or convex. The stem edges are straight and tapered. Small, weak side notches form the shoulders. The basal edge is convex or straight and is usually unfinished, but may be thinned and ground. Chipping is short, random, deep with very short and deep retouching.

Distribution: Found over much of the United States.

1.00-2.00

NATIONWIDE

MUD CREEK: 3000 to 1000 B.C.

Description: This medium size dart point has a triangular shaped blade with a sharp point and convex edges. The stem is expanded, has straight edges and tapered, rounded or right angular shoulders. The base is thinned and may be ground and the edges are straight or convex. The chipping pattern is broad, random and shallow with small, fairly deep retouching.

Distribution: Found over most of the United States.

1.00-5.00

NATIONWIDE

MULBERRY CREEK: 4500 to 1000 B.C.

Description: This is a medium to large size dart point with a lanceolate shaped blade, convex edges, a straight or tapered stem and shoulders narrow and usually tapered. The widest point on the blade is near the mid-section. Usually the base is convex, but may be straight and slightly thinned. The chipping is broad, shallow and random with fine retouching along the blade and crude retouching along the stem.

Distribution: Found over most of the United States.

5.00-15.00

NATIONWIDE

NOLAN: 4000 B.C. to 1000 A.D.

Description: This is a medium to large dart point having convex or recurved edges, barbless shoulders, and a needle sharp point. Generally, the stems are parallel or may expand or contract slightly. The base is usually straight or convex, rarely concave. There is a strong, steep bevel on the stem, rarely found on the blade. This point is fairly common.

Distribution: Found over most of the United States.

1.00-15.00

NATIONWIDE

NORMANSKILL: 3500 to 1000 B.C.

Description: This medium sized dart point has a narrow, triangular, thick blade with straight edges, slightly thinned and expanded stem and tapered shoulders. The basal edge is straight or slightly concave. There is random chipping with little retouching.

Distribution: Found over most of the United States.

1.00-5.00

NATIONWIDE

OTTER CREEK: 1 to 700 A.D.

Description: This large dart or spear point has a large, thick, lanceolate to triangular shaped blade with convex, seldom straight edges. Usually the stem is ground. Basal edge is usually concave and sometimes straight. Side notches are nicely made with square tangs. Chipping pattern is broad and random with good retouching.

Distribution: Found over all of the United States.

1.00-15.00

NATIONWIDE

PANDORA: 2000 B.C. to 1000 A.D.

Description: This medium to large sized point has a triangular to leaf-shape blade. Edges may be almost straight, usually convex. The base is straight. The usual size is 2 to 5 inches.

Distribution: Over most of the United States.

1.00-15.00

NATIONWIDE

PINE TREE: 7000 to 5000 B.C.

Description: This is a medium dart point having a lanceolate shaped blade with convex edges, expanded stem and narrow and tapered shoulders. The base is concave and thinned. Chipping is broad, shallow and random with collateral or random retouching.

Distribution: Found over most of the United States.

3.00-8.00

NATIONWIDE

SCOTTSBLUFF: 7500 to 5000 B.C.

Description: This is a medium to large size dart or spear point. The blade is broad and triangular shaped with straight to slightly convex edges and a rectangular stem. Definite shoulders cut in at right angles. The base may be ground and will be straight, or slightly concave or convex. This point is rare.

Distribution: It is found over most of the United States.

7.50-20.00

NATIONWIDE

SUBLET FERRY: 2500 to 500 B.C.

Description: This small dart point has a lanceolate to triangular shaped blade with edges that are convex and sometime tend to be parallel toward the base. Shallow side notches form the stem which is often as wide as the blade. The basal edge is straight and thin. Chipping pattern is shallow to deep & random with long, narrow retouching forming serrations along the blade edges.

Distribution: Found over all the United States.

.50-3.00

NATIONWIDE

SWAN LAKE: 3500 to 1000 B.C.

Description: This small dart point has a narrow, thick, triangular shaped blade with straight or slightly convex or concave odges, weak shoulders formed by side notches & convex or straight base. Usually the base is the widest part of the point and is often unfinished showing part of the original blank surface. Chipping is short, random with short, deep retouching.

Distribution: Found over all of the United States.

.50-2.00

NATIONWIDE

TRINITY: 2000 to 1000 B.C.

Description: This small to medium size dart point has a triangular blade with straight to convex edges. The stem is formed by two shallow notches crudely chipped into the sides near the base and has poorly developed shoulders. The basal edge is straight to convex and bulging to align with the blade edges. Sometimes the stem and base are smoothed. This point has a thick and heavy cross-section.

Distribution: Found over most of the United States.

1.00-3.00

NATIONWIDE

VOSBURG: 7000 to 5000 B.C.

Description: This medium sized dart point has a broad, thin, triangular blade with straight to slightly convex or concave edges and a short, expanding stem. Shoulders are small, notched & expanding with weak barbs. Usually the base is ground and the edges are straight or slightly concave. There is broad, shallow, random chipping with fine retouching and slight serration may be present.

Distribution: Found over most of the United States.

1.00-5.00

NATIONWIDE

WADE: 2500 to 1500 B.C.

Description: This is a medium sized dart point having a thin, triangular blade with straight to convex sides. Usually the stem is straight, but may be slightly expanded. The stem edges are straight the shoulders are strong with strong barbs. Basal edge is straight or convex, thinned and slightly ground. Chipping pattern is deep, shallow and random and the notches and stem are retouched.

Distribution: Found over most of the United States.

1.00-5.00

NATIONWIDE

WHITE SPRINGS: 5000 to 3500 B.C.

Description: This is a medium dart point having convex or occasionally straight to slightly concave edges. The blade is fairly thin and triangular shaped with a short, broad stem and small right angular shoulders. Edges of the stem are straight or may be slightly concave or convex, base thinned, and usually ground. Flaking is shallow and random. On rare occasions, there is traverse oblique chipping.

Distribution: Found over most of the United States.

1.00-8.00

NATIONWIDE

YOUNG: 1200 to 1500 A.D.

Description: This small point has a triangular to leaf shaped blade with the edges strongly convex and often asymetrical. The basal edge is straight to convex and often crooked. The point is crudely made from a curved flake with little modification, usually not enough to flatten the artifact.

Distribution: Found over a wide area of the United States.

.50-1.50